Entertainment WEEKLY

1999

Yearbook

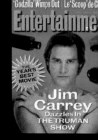

EDITOR Alison Gwinn

ART DIRECTOR Lynette Cortez for Divine Design Studio, Inc.

PICTURE EDITOR Sarah Rozen

DEPUTY EDITORS Matthew McCann Fenton,
Jamie Malanowski

ASSOCIATE EDITORS Bianca Perlman, Dalton Ross,
Charles Runnette

ASSOCIATE ART DIRECTORS Jennie Chang, Tonya Hudson,
Ellene Wundrok

ASSISTANT PICTURE EDITORS Deborah Dragon,
Freyda C. Tavin

PICTURE RESEARCHER Luciana Chang

REPORTERS Carmela Ciuraru, Melinda Dodd,
Kristi Huelsing, Beth Johnson, Allyssa Lee, Karen Mancuso,
Leslie Marable, Tim Purtell, Joshua Rich, Erin Richter,
Nancy Sidewater, Daneet Steffens, Lori L. Tharps,
Amy Weaver

EDITORIAL PRODUCTION MANAGER David M. Serrano

COPY CHIEF Ben Spier

DEPUTY COPY CHIEF Alexandria Dionne

COPY EDITORS Mila Drumke,
Cynthia McClean, David Penick

TIME INC. HOME ENTERTAINMENT

PRESIDENT David Gitow

DIRECTOR, CONTINUITIES AND SINGLE SALES David Arfine

DIRECTOR, CONTINUITIES AND RETENTION Michael Barrett

DIRECTOR, NEW PRODUCTS Alicia Longobardo

GROUP PRODUCT MANAGERS Robert Fox, Jennifer McLyman

PRODUCT MANAGERS Christopher Berzolla,
Roberta Harris, Stacy Hirschberg, Kenneth Maehlum,
Daniel Melore

MANAGER, RETAIL AND NEW MARKETS Thomas Mifsud

ASSOCIATE PRODUCT MANAGERS Carlos Jimenez,
Daria Raehse, Betty Su, Niki Viswanathan,
Lauren Zaslansky, Cheryl Zukowski

ASSISTANT PRODUCT MANAGERS Jennifer Dowell,
Meredith Shelley

EDITORIAL OPERATIONS DIRECTOR John Calvano

BOOK PRODUCTION MANAGER Jessica McGrath

ASSISTANT BOOK PRODUCTION MANAGER Joseph Napolitano

FULFILLMENT DIRECTOR Michelle Gudema

ASSISTANT FULFILLMENT MANAGER Richard Perez

FINANCIAL DIRECTOR Tricia Griffin

FINANCIAL MANAGER Amy Maselli

ASSISTANT FINANCIAL MANAGER Steven Sandonato

MARKETING ASSISTANT Ann Gillespie

Special thanks to Anna Yelenskaya

HARDCOVER ISBN: 1-883013-58-5
ISSN: 1097-5705

We welcome your comments and suggestions about Entertainment Weekly Books. Please write to us at: ENTERTAINMENT WEEKLY Books, Attention: Book Editors, PO Box 11016, Des Moines, IA 50336-1016.

If you would like to order any of our Hardcover Collector Edition books, please call us at 1-800-327-6388 (Monday through Friday, 7 a.m.–8 p.m., or Saturday, 7 a.m.–6 p.m., Central Time).

GELLAR: PHOTOGRAPH BY NORMAN JEAN ROY; AGENCY: EDGE; STYLING: DANIEL CAUDILL/VISAGES; HAIR: CRAIG GANJI/HELLER; MAKEUP: SHARON GAULT/NARS/ARTIST GROUP MGMT.; SLIP: BARNEYS NY; BRA: MAIDENFORM. HANKS: PHOTOGRAPH BY PEGGY SIROTA; RUSSELL. PHOTOGRAPH BY NORMAN JEAN ROY; AGENCY: EDGE; STYLING: DANIEL CAUDILL/VISAGES; HAIR: DAVID GARDNER/VISAGES; MAKEUP: MAITAL SAB BAN/VISAGES; ROBERTS: PHOTOGRAPH BY MATTHEW ROLSTON

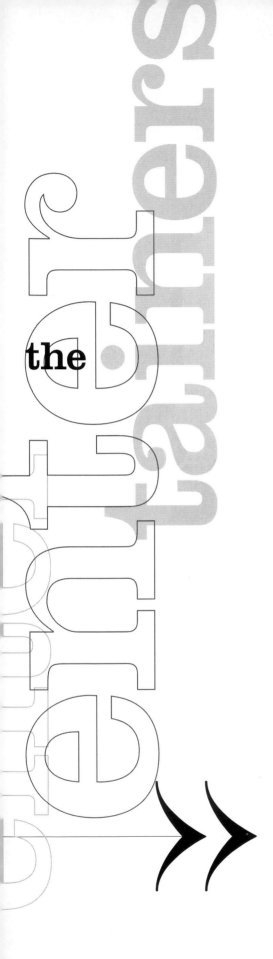

the entertainers

Miseducated was Lauryn Hill,

Though she seemed awfully smart to us;

Bridget worried about adding poundage,

But Calista's loss caused all the fuss.

The box office swelled for Adam's movies—

All for him was peachy,

But the darling of the independents

Was sweet 'n' sour Christina Ricci.

Hanks and Spielberg hit the beach—

Private Ryan sure was scary

And made us all even queasier

Than the Farrellys could about *Mary*.

Audiences would likely go anywhere

When Shania sang "Come On Over,"

Though if *anywhere* was Fontana's *Oz*,

They'd be too freaked out to bother.

The kids liked the strutting Backstreet Boys—

AJ, Brian, Kevin, Nick, and Howie Sweet D—

Though they looked like they'd be eaten alive

By the girls of The WB.

But Leonardo's fans were the most devoted;

They bought tickets by the score:

Every time that boat went down

They loved him all the more.

These were the year's best entertainers;

We loved you much and greatly.

But before you get too comfy, folks—

What have you done for us lately?

leonardo caprio

CONSIDER HIS DUAL ROLE IN *THE MAN IN THE IRON MASK*; add to that his terrific bit of self-parody in Woody Allen's *Celebrity*; then tally the grosses for a certain boat movie that sailed through the first quarter of 1998 and left box office records in its wake. Factor them all together, and they still won't explain why Leonardo DiCaprio is ENTERTAINMENT WEEKLY's 1998 Entertainer of the Year. For DiCaprio—or rather, the phenomenon of DiCaprio—is much greater than the sum of his accomplishments. In 1998, for better or worse, he came to personify the unique era and culture that declared him a star. The 24-year-old actor (a really fine actor, lest we forget) grew so large on the global cultural landscape that he was recognized by one name: LEO—two vowels and one consonant typed incessantly by headline writers whose publications chronicled his every business dealing (one day he's starring in *American Psycho*, the next he's not); his every foray into nightclubs; his every alleged canoodle with a model (Kate! Amber! Naomi!). DiCaprio's lack of an Oscar nod for *Titanic*, and his subsequent no-show at the March event, got more attention than anyone who *did* show. Internet enthusiasts could visit 500 websites to declare their love for Leo or join in the inevitable backlash. Book publishers searched for the soul behind the night crawler in tomes such as *Lovin' Leo: Your Leonardo DiCaprio Keepsake Scrapbook* and *Leonardo DiCaprio: Romantic Hero*. ● And amid the sound and fury of Leo-mania (a frenzy, by the way, unparalleled since the Beatles), the object of all this affection kept a carefully choreographed distance. By relaying "no comment" or speaking through his beleaguered publicist, DiCaprio revealed nothing about himself; meanwhile, he spoke volumes about us. The box office figures of *Titanic* ($1.8 billion worldwide) and the Internet hours devoted to its star signified the power of the exploding post-boom teen audience, with money to burn and an insatiable hunger for pop culture. America's fascination with movie stars—which DiCaprio sent up in *Celebrity* by playing a bratty, fawned-over young actor—was accommodated with torrents of ink and gales of airtime: Leo goes house hunting! Leo visits a fan in the hospital! Leo has a dozen TVs! And attaches Sony PlayStations to each one! ● If 1998 was the year of non-news (a year in which the media were held captive by the White House intern affair), then Leo was its poster boy. While the poster girl wore a beret and a navy dress, Leo wore a leather jacket and stared from the magazine racks—floppy-haired, glassy-eyed, and tight-lipped, the portrait of the artist as a young commodity. ● It has been said more than once—more than a hundred times, in fact—that in 1996 DiCaprio nearly lost his life in a sky-diving incident. Without his instructor there to pull the emergency cord, our words devoted to Leo would have mourned the passing of a good son (he's close to his mother) and an actor whose potential would never be fully realized. (DiCaprio had already received an Oscar nomination for 1993's *What's Eating Gilbert Grape*.) But as it happens, you can almost imagine Leo, alive and well and channel-surfing in front of one of his alleged dozen TV sets, catching a glimpse of himself on *Hard Copy*, and wondering "Was I spared for this?" We find ourselves worried about his future, questioning whether he can outlive his superstardom and emerge as an artist when fame tends to stunt the growth of all but its wisest recipients. ● After months of post-*Titanic* speculation, DiCaprio has finally cast his eye toward two projects, neither of which suggests he's playing it safe. He's expressed interest in portraying dark-souled jazz musician Chet Baker in an in-development biopic for Miramax. And in January, shooting began on *The Beach,* directed by *Trainspotting*'s Danny Boyle and based on a 1997 Alex Garland novel about an island utopia. DiCaprio will play a nomadic dreamer looking for paradise. ● Will he find it? No comment, not yet. —JESS CAGLE

1

hanks

THERE ARE CERTAIN RARE HISTORICAL OCCURRENCES like Halley's comet that should be cherished when they swing by. The same is true in a celestial realm closer to home—namely, the galaxy of Hollywood. How often do we get to see a generation's greatest director and leading man team up? Every 20 years...if we're lucky? In the '40s and early '50s, John Huston and Humphrey Bogart joined forces for *The Maltese Falcon, The Treasure of the Sierra Madre*, and *The African Queen*. In the '70s and early '80s, Martin Scorsese and Robert De Niro gave us *Mean Streets, Taxi Driver*, and *Raging Bull*. In 1998, in what we hope will be a far more frequent occurrence than Professor Halley's fantasia, Steven Spielberg and Tom Hanks converged in *Saving Private Ryan*. Both Spielberg, 52, and Hanks, 42, have topped this list before (Spielberg in '93, Hanks in '94). But their epic meditation on D-Day raised the bar. From the film's frenzied, gut-wrenching opening on Omaha Beach, we knew this wouldn't be our fathers' WWII movie. Soldiers muttered Hail Marys and heaved over the sides of their Higgins boats; waves crashing on the Normandy shore became a horrifying red tide; and the very concept of fearlessness in fighting "the Good War" was overshadowed by the existential meat grinder that was June 6, 1944. "D-Day was the turning point of the 20th century. Those few minutes are like a microcosm of our century—the waist of the hourglass," says *Ryan* producer Gary Levinsohn. "Finding important stories to tell is hard, but finding the right way to tell them is even harder." The team of Spielberg and Hanks made it look easy—and the resulting film went on to pull in a staggering $190 million at the box office. • If *Schindler's List* was Spielberg's rite of passage from starry-eyed man-child to a more serious filmmaker, then *Ryan* showed him making good on that promise. Just as Sam Peckinpah and Sergio Leone turned the Westerns of John Ford on their head—replacing the flawless hero with the morally blurry Everyman—Spielberg performed a revelatory feat of revisionism with *Ryan*, showing us a WWII that looked (and even seemed to smell) like hell. • At the center of the century-defining tempest is Hanks' Captain Miller. There's a reason the actor is compared to Jimmy Stewart: Hanks too excels at playing the supremely decent man overwhelmed by circumstance. And in Spielberg, Hanks found his Hitchcock. He could have pulled off a cardboard hero in his sleep; but in Miller's trembling hands and ashen grimace, we see a man at war not only with Germans but with his conscience—a rational officer trying to make sense of irrational surroundings. • Hanks later returned to his aw-shucks romantic-comedy stomping grounds in *You've Got Mail*. But he and Spielberg will continue to grapple with WWII in a 13-hour miniseries they will exec-produce for HBO (slated for late 2000). Still, it's hard to imagine their small-screen venture will carry the emotional bang of *Ryan*. "I was aware that I was involved in something that was much bigger than the sum of its parts," Hanks said. "But I didn't really know what I'd been involved in until Steven showed it to me. And I was emotionally crippled by it. I sat in the car for 20 minutes afterwards. I couldn't drive." Join the club. —CHRIS NASHAWATY/PHOTOGRAPH BY NORMAN JEAN ROY

AGENCY: EDGE; STYLING: DANIEL CAUDILL/VISAGES; GROOMING: HELEN JEFFERS/CLOUTIER; SPIELBERG'S SHIRT: TOMMY HILFIGER; HANKS' CLOTHES: GIORGIO ARMANI

even spielberg

the girls

(From left)
Combs, Williams, Biel, Holmes, Gellar, Doherty, Russell, Milano

AND TO THINK, ONLY TWO years ago, the most famous pair of legs on The WB belonged to the network's corporate mascot, Michigan J. Frog. • Then Sarah Michelle Gellar's *Buffy the Vampire Slayer* kicked down the door for strong young women on TV. Soon *7th Heaven*'s Jessica Biel, 16; *Dawson's Creek*'s Katie Holmes, 20, and Michelle Williams, 18; *Charmed*'s Shannen Doherty, 27, Alyssa Milano, 26, and Holly Marie Combs, 25; and *Felicity*'s Keri Russell, 22, joined Gellar, 21, as WB poster girls, attracting legions of young female fans and millions in ad revenue. Suddenly a struggling network had an identity, and Hollywood a burning obsession. • Studio execs lusting after young women? Nothing new there. Resting the fate of an entire network on their collective shoulders, however, *is* new. And The WB—one of the few networks to see Nielsen growth in the 1998-99 season thanks to its young viewers (the net says two thirds of its audience is under 35)—has cornered the market on smart, youth-directed, female-driven programming. "Twelve- to 34-year-olds view women differently," explains WB entertainment president Garth Ancier. "They've grown up in a world where women are more empowered. We're reflecting that world." • Ironically, these characters seem more competent and confident than their older sisters on other networks, neurotic career women such as Ally McBeal and Veronica Chase. Biel's Mary "is a good student who can take on any guy in basketball and win," says Ancier; Williams' Jen and Holmes' Joey are growing up without parents; Russell's freshman Felicity is making it on her own in New York. • So the WB girls are positive role models. But don't underestimate the power of the superficial: They're also smokin' hotties. "*Charmed* is a perfect postfeminist girl-power show," says Milano, one of its three witch sibs. "These women are strong, but they're still feminine and accessible." • Alert to the scent of money, moviemakers have tapped The WB's girl-power gold mine, snapping up Gellar for *Scream 2* and *I Know What You Did Last Summer*, Holmes for *Disturbing Behavior*, and Williams for *Halloween: H20*. Coming attractions include Russell's Irish romance *Perfect Timing*, Williams' Nixon-era comedy *Dick*, Holmes' revenge fantasy *Killing Mrs. Tingle*, and *Cruel Intentions*, an adolescent retelling of *Dangerous Liaisons* with the WB all-star team of Gellar, *Creek*'s Joshua Jackson, and Selma Blair (whose midseason series about a New York teen, *Zoe Bean*, aims to bring The WB's female formula to sitcoms). • Of course, *Party of Five*'s Neve Campbell and Jennifer Love Hewitt also made the leap to movies, but their TV aliases continue to mope, while The WB's women are kicking butt, both figuratively and (in Gellar's case) literally. "They're all fighters," observes Russell. "They're not sitting in their pink bedrooms with their teddy bears. They're exploring and experiencing life." You go, WB girls. —BRUCE FRETTS/PHOTOGRAPH BY NORMAN JEAN ROY

of the

DIGITAL COMPOSITE: NORMAN JEAN ROY; AGENCY: EDGE; STYLING: DANIEL CAUDILL/VISAGES; SET STYLING: PETER GARGAGLIANO/VISAGES; HAIR: DAVID GARDNER/VISAGES; GELLAR'S HAIR: CRAIG GANJI/HELLER; COMBS' MAKEUP: KAREN YOSHIMOTO/CELESTINE; WILLIAMS' AND HOLMES' MAKEUP: SCOTT PATRIC/GARREN NY; BIEL'S AND GELLAR'S MAKEUP: SHARON GAULT/NARS/ARTIST GROUP MGMT.; DOHERTY'S MAKEUP: VICTOR JOSEPH/CLOUTIER; RUSSELL'S MAKEUP: MAITAL SABBAN/VISAGES; MILANO'S MAKEUP: PATRICK DE FONTBRUNE/SHU UEMURA/CELESTINE; CORSETS: UPTIGHT CORSETS; BRAS: MAIDENFORM; COMBS' SKIRT: GIORGIO ARMANI; WILLIAMS', HOLMES', AND MILANO'S SKIRTS: DANIEL CAUDILL; BIEL'S SKIRT: MONAH LI; GELLAR'S SKIRT: RICHARD TYLER; GELLAR'S SLIP: BARNEYS NY; DOHERTY'S SKIRT: AMY MICHAELSON; RUSSELL'S DRESS: DOLCE & GABBANA

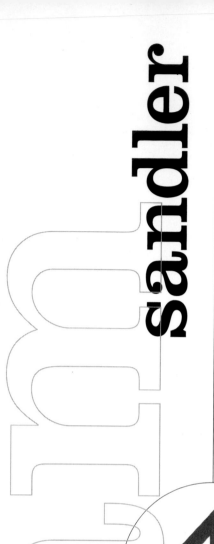

adam sandler

4

OH, ADAM! SILLY, DERANGED ADAM. What on earth is your momma gonna do with you? Spouting crazy gibberish to imaginary penguins. Howling like a wounded wildebeest and tackling your teachers to the floor. Picking fights with Bob Barker. Who told you this was an acceptable way for a 32-year-old to act? • Millions of sniggering accomplices, that's who. Thanks to not one but two blockbuster movies, *The Wedding Singer* and *The Waterboy*, 1998 was the year Sandler—a human spitball in the eye of sophistication and taste—sailed to the head of the comedy class. And definitely it was the year when his matted-down Brillo 'do and goofed-out grin landed on comedy's Mount Rushmore, right next to the crumbling visage of Jim Carrey's talking butt cheeks. • That's not to say this was a shock to anyone but the unconverted. Since breaking out on *Saturday Night Live* with freakazoid flair (who could forget Cajun Man or Opera Man?), Sandler has assembled a frat-brat fan base through such lunkheaded flicks as *Billy Madison* and *Happy Gilmore*. His gimmick is as simple as his characters: Young man boasting the emotional intelligence of a blow-dryer gets sucked into trouble, yet manages to dumb his way to redemption. "There's just something really safe and likable about seeing this guy up there," observes his *SNL* bud David Spade. "Even if you're only 5 years old, you poke your friend and say, 'At least I'm not as dumb as that idiot!' " • The critics would certainly second that. "His existence in our cultural consciousness implies intellectual sloth of previously unimagined proportions," sniffed *Newsday* in its *Madison* review. To which the incredibly highbrow *New York Post* added that Sandler "is a staggeringly untalented waste of space." What, you think falling over while trying to whizz into a kiddie urinal is easy? • Admittedly, no one's confusing our man-child du jour with Buster Keaton (the press-allergic star couldn't care less about legitimacy, anyway). But *The Wedding Singer* at least offered evidence of a broader appeal—even a wink of semiserious acting! Playing a shlubby entertainer who falls for an already engaged waitress (Drew Barrymore), Sandler toned down the potty humor, turned up the charm, and earned glowing reviews. Box office receipts quickly followed—to the tune of $80 million—transforming his off-kilter dunce cap into a crown shimmering with mainstream acceptance. • Longtime Sandler fans may have scratched their heads a bit: Was the Duke of Dork letting the air out of his whoopee cushion? But relief came soon enough, with *Waterboy*'s half-wit cracker Bobby Boucher. In this demented tale of one freak's unquenchable devotion to football, his momma, and, you know, *water*, Sandler was back in blockheaded bliss: whimpering like a disturbed child, hurling his body all over the screen, and feel-gooding us into a bumbling heroic climax. Critics were right there to sack him, of course, but what better defense than *Waterboy*'s $130 million-plus box office touchdown and a two-picture deal with New Line worth more than $35 million? In Sandler's upcoming Columbia project, *Big Daddy*, he'll examine the nuances of parenthood, as a dude who adopts a kid to impress his girlfriend. • "I think we're just getting started with the adventures of Adam," predicts Chris Rock, another *SNL* pal. "The first movie was Adam goes back to school. Then Adam plays hockey and golf. Adam falls in love. Adam plays football. Now Adam's a dad. Next...he goes to the moon. Yeah, Sandler saves the world!" • Not a bad idea. After all, it's Sandler's world now—we just laugh in it. —DAN SNIERSON

calista

IT MAY NOT SEEM OBVIOUS ON THE SURFACE, but it is without a doubt true that the anger, the annoyance, the sheer outpouring of spleen that has been directed this year toward Calista (Greek for "Most Beautiful") Flockhart and her on-screen alter ego Ally McBeal is in fact a testimony to the actress' great attractiveness and the deep appeal of her character. After all, nothing exasperates us quite so much as the people and things we love. And the more we root for, feel tenderly toward, or identify with the winsome, vulnerable title character of Fox's two-season-old hit, the more galling we find her inappropriately abbreviated skirts, her quivering, gaunt demeanor. ● As if that weren't enough, we then feel free to take issue with what we think this creation of a man—exec producer David E. Kelley—represents. TIME held up Ally McBeal as the symbol of young, modern, sexually liberated women who seem to want to distance themselves from feminism, and as the sad end product of the struggles of Susan B. Anthony and Gloria Steinem. A few months later, it was the real Flockhart who was under the microscope, or at least her too-prominent clavicle and scapula were, as the nation eagerly digressed from matters Lewinsky to debate the possibility of Flockhart's eating disorder and if she was presenting a poor role model for young women. These top-of-the-news discussions required a cover story denial from Flockhart, after which the great media beast turned its attention elsewhere. ● It's the province of certain real-seeming shows to twist us up this way; think of *thirtysomething*, and how everything about it was so appealingly real until it thudded into an iceberg of "Who Would Do *That*?" But Kelley's conceit, for all its quirky verisimilitude, is as much a fantasy as the Bionic Woman; picking at the absurd unbelievability of things like the law firm's unisex bathroom or nightly socializing is as logical as pooh-poohing the biotechnical underpinnings of Jaime Sommers' amazing powers. It misses the point: *Ally McBeal* is a Rorschach test, and what's being tested is the viewer's ideas of sex, power, and young womanhood; the question ought not to be "Why does she act that way?" but, more profitably, "Why do I?" ● And Flockhart, 34, is the perfect actress to provoke this sort of inquiry. Like an island limned with bays and inlets and bordered with broad beaches, her wide, undisguising eyes and sensual, tremulous mouth offer visitors easy points of access to the character's lively inner life. It must be hard playing a character so purposely unformed—though perhaps not harder than being scrutinized both for what you do *and* what your character does. Flockhart just tries to focus on the positives. "I feel very fortunate—I get to come to work every day and act, and in a good part that has controversies and complexities. I certainly don't worry about people liking Ally. The fact that some people like her and some people don't like her gives me a lot of freedom as an actress to do whatever I want. It's a big playing field I have, and it's nice to know there are no rules." ● No rules? What an enviable position! Of course, it's the reality of rules, and watching Ally figure out which ones to bend, or break, or make, that keeps us tuning in. —JAMIE MALANOWSKI

"*SOMETIMES YOU MEET GIRLS and they recognize you, but they won't say anything. They'll just giggle and scream and laugh and then just run away. I pray to God I get inside a girl's head one day and see, What in the WORLD are they thinking?"* ● *So speaks Backstreet Boy AJ McLean, 21. And he brings up an excellent question. Not being teenage girls ourselves, we can't be absolutely sure what goes on inside those adolescent skulls. But here's an educated guess*: Omigod! I'm totally gonna pee in my pants. Right now. I'm gonna *pee* in my pants! AJ is standing right in front of me. He's sooo hot. But also a little scary, ya know? 'Cause he's the bad boy. He's got lotsa piercings and also a tattoo of a panda. Pandas are his favorite. God, I can't believe I forgot to bring the stuffed panda! That totally sucks. My mom says it was a waste of money. But she doesn't like my BSB posters or scrapbook or bandannas or pillows or unauthorized biographies, either. She's got no clue. Neither does my boyfriend. He'll listen to them but thinks they're gay. Yeah, right. He *wishes*! ● Oh, AJ! *I'll* Quit Playing Games With Your Heart. That's the Boys' *best* song. I could listen to it a zillion times! I read that their CD—*Backstreet Boys*—sold, like, 25 million copies around the world. It's the third-best-selling album of the year, after the *Titanic* soundtrack and Celine Dion's album. Oh, Leo, Leo, Leo. No! *Focus!* It's AJ I love. ● *Am I sexual?* AJ, you don't have to ask! Okay, so I'm not. But I would be for him. You know who else I'd be sexual for? Some of those other hottie boy bands that copy BSB: 'N Sync. Five. Code Red. Dru Hill. Did I mention 'N Sync? Justin is *gorgeous*! Okay, focus again. Need to stay loyal. BSB was my first love. They were the originals; the others are just wannabes. ● Omigod! That girl over there just gave AJ her bra! I wish I'd thought of that—I'd give it to Nick. He's my *real* fave BSB 'cause we've got lots in common. We're both Aquarians, we both love videogames, and he's 19, so more my age. Nick once said: "Everyone wants a girl with a perfect personality. It doesn't really matter how they look." He wouldn't mind my braces or...*ooooh*, there's Kevin! He's kinda old—like 26. But that's okay. I read in *Teen Beat* he's a "real softy" who'll cry over anything. He said he's "bashful.... I like it when a girl tells me she likes me." I like you! I like you! But I'd even go out with 25-year-old Howie—Sweet D, I call him, 'cause he's the nicest—or 23-year-old Brian (B-Rok). He hates green vegetables. Me, too! Let's not eat veggies together, Brian! ● My older sister says the Backstreet Boys are just a fad, like when she used to listen to the New Kids on the Block. As if! Okay, so they both had the same manager. But, BSB can *sing*. Even my teacher—and she's *really* old—thinks they're talented. Also, they're amazing dancers. Okay, the New Kids could dance too, but BSB are a *million* times cuter. They're more like that band my mom liked, the one with Sean Lennon's dad. —A.J. JACOBS/PHOTOGRAPH BY ANDREW SOUTHAM

6

reet

WHAT'S THE MOST UNFORGETTABLE IMAGE OF '98? Could it be John Glenn saluting from the shuttle? Mark McGwire swatting his 62nd homer? Dr. Kevorkian doing his thing on *60 Minutes*? Nah. The most indelible visual had to be Ben Stiller's nether parts stuck in a zipper. Try as we might, we just can't erase that repulsive, wince-inducing close-up from *There's Something About Mary*. Of course, why would we want to? The shot was downright hilarious. And for that, we can thank the brothers Farrelly. • With *Mary*, cowriters and directors Peter and Bobby became the undisputed Visionaries of Vulgarity, the Kings of Crass. Admittedly, it's a prize they've had their eyes on for years. First came their 1994 megahit *Dumb & Dumber* (lots of snot and poop humor), then their less successful—though thankfully no less revolting—follow-up, 1996's *Kingpin* (in which the Farrellys graduated to vomit and bull semen). But with last summer's R-rated charmer, the siblings hit new highs—and lows. The genius of *Mary*? It manages to be a heart-tugging romance—snaring a whole new class of Farrelly fan (namely, female)—while upping the stomach-churning gags: Need we mention the old lady swapping spit with her Border terrier? Or Cameron Diaz applying a certain protein-rich hair gel? Prim and proper folks may have smelled the apocalypse, but the rest of us ate it up. *Mary*'s domestic gross: $173 million. • "It's been a gas," says Bobby (right), summing up the year with an appropriately flatulent metaphor. "People are trained to think we'd never go as far as we do. So the surprise is funny. If everyone starts doing it, which I'm sure they will, it might not be as funny." • In fact, everyone has *already* started doing it. Even before Diaz's seminal 'do, *South Park* and Adam Sandler were busy offending America's sensibilities. But it was *Mary*'s unexpected killing at the summer box office that sent the signal to the world: Wordy smart aleck Jerry Seinfeld has left the zeitgeist. Welcome to the Age of Adolescent Entertainment! • No doubt the nation's appetite for all things tasteless will eventually subside. But for now, Peter and Bobby (41 and 40, respectively) are flush with success. This after they spent a decade selling unproduced screenplays (15, to be exact), and Bobby struck out as an inventor (his circular beach towel—so you don't have to shift it when the sun moves—didn't exactly fly off the shelves). Next up for the sibling auteurs: *Stuck on You*, a Siamese-twin comedy featuring Woody Allen and a yet-to-be-named costar. "In no way are we making fun of Siamese twins," promises the ever-sensitive Bobby. "We love these characters." • Sounds intriguingly ludicrous. Still, it'll be hard to top Ben Stiller's bloody crotch. Which, we should point out, wasn't actually Stiller's. For the infamous close-up, the Farrellys ordered a four-foot-tall zipper and a kickball-size gonad. Sadly, the zipper broke, and the brothers had to take the scary-looking contraption to a local tailor to be fixed. The poor fellow practically had a heart attack. "That's the mark of good comedy," Bobby says, "when you've got people almost dying." Consider us slain. —AJJ/
PHOTOGRAPH BY MICHAEL GRECCO

the
farrelly
brothers

Lauryn Hill

8

YOU CAN ALMOST HEAR THE SQUEAL OF THE NAYSAYERS. "Lauryn, sweetheart, you're making a big mistake. Now is *not* the time to go solo. Now is *not* the time to have a baby. Now is *not* the time for real live musical instruments—I mean, what do you think this is, Stax in the '60s? And for chrissakes, now is *not* the time to have *another* baby." ● Thanks to some deep strain of confidence or chutzpah, Lauryn Hill decided not to listen. In a marketplace that considers focus-group feedback more useful than instinct—a world in which songs sell movies and movies sell cheeseburgers—the female Fugee wrote and produced *The Miseducation of Lauryn Hill*, a demographic-defying, expectation-bucking hybrid of island and street, Muscle Shoals and Def Jam and Tuff Gong, vinegar-laced hip-hop screeds and honey-drizzled R&B madrigals. "I wanted to experiment in sound," she says. "I didn't want it to be too technically perfect." From a niche-marketing standpoint, it made no sense. It debuted at the top of *Billboard*'s album chart anyway and had sold 3 million copies by year's end. ● *Miseducation* also turned Hill, 23, into the year's critical darling, in a league with rock-press fixtures like Beck and Radiohead. Which is sort of hard to fathom, if you look back. Only two years ago, Hill was shaping up to be a gorgeous answer to a future trivia question: "Which actress from *As the World Turns* sang on the Fugees' remake of Roberta Flack's 'Killing Me Softly With His Song' in 1996?" Yet just when the Fugees looked to be turning into their inevitable punchline—"the luckiest wedding band on the planet"—Hill stopped copying the classics and created a dozen of her own. Carlos Santana, the Woodstock Generation ax slinger who dropped in for a cameo on *Miseducation*'s "To Zion," says that Hill is "proving to the world that quality and quantity can dance together." ● "To Zion," in fact, feels like the heart of *Miseducation*. The song is Hill's tribute to her infant son, Zion, but it's also a snarled snap back at those who advised her not to have him. "I knew his life deserved a chance," she simmers, "but everybody told me to be smart/'Look at your career,' they said/'Lauryn, baby, use your head'/But instead I chose to use my heart." (And yes, she's still making that choice: In November Hill gave birth to daughter Selah Louise, her second bambino with boyfriend and reggae scion Rohan Marley.) "When I heard the song, it broke me up," Santana says. "Especially when she says that the whole world is telling her, 'Man, what are you *doing* getting pregnant? You're at the peak of the game! You're at the peak of your career!' The world says you should be doing *this*, and the record company says you should be doing *this*. But your heart says, 'Go this way,' so you go that way. It takes a lot of courage to do that." ● "I was listening to Nina Simone and Stevie Wonder records back in the day and feeling 'Oh, God!' and wanting to cry," Hill says. "So when you have people telling you 'This made me cry' or 'Girl, you wrote that song for me,' it makes me feel like I'm moving in the right direction. Beyond what the critics say. Beyond what the industry says. What the *people* say." To paraphrase yet another poet from the old school, Lauryn Hill took the road less traveled in 1998. And that made all the difference. —JEFF GORDINIER

DISMEMBERMENT, CRUCIFIXION, RAPE...NOW, THAT'S ENTERTAINMENT! Or so it was for eight gloriously grotesque hours last summer, as the second season of Tom Fontana's HBO series, *Oz*, gave us something to sweat about. ● Emerald City, Oswald Penitentiary's segregated experimental unit, was a universe unto itself. But if Judy Garland's fever-dreamed never-never land was a foray into heavenly bliss, Fontana's creation was a perverse, horrific journey from which no amount of heel clicking was gonna bring you back. ● What brought viewers back was their own eager anticipation: Would Milquetoasty "punk" Beecher finally go medieval on his Nazi tormentor, Schillinger? Who would be the next target of Ryan O'Reilly's lone-wolf savagery? And what was Adebisi keeping under that precariously perched hat? But while *Oz* was hands down the most testosterone-fueled series on the air, its enmeshed plot arcs, the ever-shifting loyalties among its inmates, and their ingrained amorality suggested a daytime soap—an analogy the 47-year-old Fontana wholeheartedly endorses: "It's a heightened world, but a reflection of the world we live in. It's real, yet it's unreal." ● *Oz*'s brilliantly realized milieu, in which the horrendous is made mundane (and vice versa), is a vision Fontana has honed for seven seasons as executive producer of NBC's *Homicide: Life on the Street*. From the Baltimore squad's watershed battle with drug lord Luther Mahoney to the stately departure of star Andre Braugher (who finally scored a best actor Emmy), last season's *Homicide* served up compelling crime stories. Perhaps most gripping of all: the Peabody award-winning "The Subway," a white-knuckled masterpiece featuring a luckless commuter (Vincent D'Onofrio) trapped beneath a subway car, his freedom attainable only at the cost of his life. Recalling *Homicide*'s genesis, Fontana offers a glimpse into his own sense of freedom: Executive producer Barry Levinson "wanted a show about thinking cops with no car chases and no gun battles. I thought, This man is completely insane—so I guess I have to go do it with him." ● In fact, both Fontana's series make an art out of defying TV convention. "I have to put challenges down for myself," he says, "because God knows the medium doesn't." Ignoring the star system and flashy atmospherics, he opts for democratic ensembles, viscerally satisfying scripts, and fly-on-the-wall visual clarity. With nary a shadow or misty-aired mise-en-scène to be found, it's life under the glare of fluorescent light—and a beacon of true inspiration. —MIKE FLAHERTY/PHOTOGRAPH BY ETHAN HILL

christina ricci

IT'S BEEN NEARLY A DECADE since a 10-year-old Christina Ricci first opened her huge, knowing peepers on screen as Winona Ryder's little sister in *Mermaids*. But in 1998, it was our turn to be wide-eyed. The girl went and grew up. And her transformation still has us reeling. ● Provocative as it was, Ricci's role as a sexually curious teen in 1997's *The Ice Storm* was just a peek at what was to come. Last May, she graduated once and for all from the *Casper*s of her early career, delivering a performance so heartless and cunning, she could give Linda Tripp a few pointers. Here's how *The Opposite of Sex* opens: Ricci's Dedee Truitt throws a cigarette into the fresh grave of her stepfather...and oh, what a roller coaster of rage follows. Thanks to Ricci, her boyfriend-stealing, murdering, just-plain-bad-to-the-bone Dedee was 1998's blackest comic gem. "I really cannot imagine anybody else in that role," says director Don Roos. "But before she auditioned I didn't even know she was old enough for it." ● Ricci's patented world-weariness began ripening as Wednesday in the *Addams Family* films. "She's done a lot of racy things, but it hasn't seemed like a total shock because she always played these mature, cynical kids," says her *Sex* costar Lisa Kudrow. The difference, of course, is in the blossoming of other charms: Full-figured Ricci stands as a refreshing antidote to the hardbodies Hollywood usually favors. More critically, she's developed a fearless instinct for off-center parts. Most of her 1998 films— *Sex*, *Buffalo 66*, *Fear and Loathing in Las Vegas*, and *Pecker*—have benefited from both her idiosyncratic beauty and her ability to embody the truly eccentric. ● No wonder she's stolen the indie-girl crown from Parker Posey. And no wonder it's so easy to forget she's a proven mainstream star. Yet despite half a life spent in Hollywood, Ricci has turned out to be both admirably unaffected and curiously, well, 18. "It came out that she's a fan of *Friends* and wanted to come visit the set," recalls Kudrow. "That surprised me. I was expecting this girl who was too cool for TV." That kind of youthful excitability is a trait Ricci rarely shows the press. Asked whether she's thrilled by her popularity, Ricci insists she's actually daunted. "In the past, I sort of did my thing and nobody paid that much attention. Now it's like every decision apparently is very important," she says, before flying off to London to play Johnny Depp's love interest in Tim Burton's *Sleepy Hollow*. Maybe she's a bit happier than she lets on? "She met Johnny Depp when she did *Mermaids* and he was Winona Ryder's boyfriend," says Roos. "So she's sort of grown into [getting] her older sister's boyfriend. She's thrilled." —DEGEN PENER/PHOTOGRAPH BY DAN WINTERS

shania

DON'T HATE HER BECAUSE SHE'S BEAUTIFUL. Hate her, if you must, because she's beautiful, personable, and writes a helluva pop song. But prepare to be outvoted: By rustling up the rural grrrl-power contingent *and* their lust-struck husbands, Twain's album *Come On Over* has gone seven-times platinum; she racked up more American Music Award nominations than any other hitmaker in 1998; and she may already be the most popular female country singer ever. If she keeps this up, Shania looks to be ever the Twain we'll meet. • Those of us who are suckers for a good hook will be fine with that, even if country traditionalists believe she's the Antichrist preincarnated as Ann-Margret. Touchy demurrals aside, nearly every one of the 16 songs on her third album is a single-in-waiting. The last hope of naysayers was that live shows would be her Achilles' heel, since she hadn't performed a single gig behind her 11-times-platinum sophomore effort, 1995's *The Woman in Me*. But when she finally toured last summer, we got something like a female Garth, albeit with more exposed midriff and less messianic hubris. "The irony of all those suspicions is that the stage is where I started," says Twain, 33, recalling her days covering hits in her native Canada. "I have most of my experience there, not video and TV." It shows, in her Brooksian ability to make everyone in an arena feel like they've been waved to by night's end. "To be honest, I'd be more nervous having a dinner party than I am entertaining 15,000 people a night." • Of course, not many dinner hosts would dress in Twain's formfitting outfits. But there's something old-fashioned about her sex appeal, which she explains in nearly neo-feminist terms: "Even on the sex symbol side of things, I'm very careful not to be sexual. I wish I had someone when I was 13 say, 'You can wear things that are flattering. You don't have to be afraid your body is changing. But do it on a comfortable level.'" • It may be her glamour, and her good humor, that lets her sneak in such female-centric messages—which she calls "a playful approach to the way I think about being a girl. It's not about feminism; it's about how awkward life is for men and women and what our roles are." • That approach plays as well in pop as in country: "You're Still the One" is already an anniversary standard. The rockier tunes, meanwhile, occasionally resemble the best of Def Leppard (old clients of husband/producer Mutt Lange). This might irk Nashville, but Twain says, "I haven't moved away from country and I don't intend to." So love her, if you dare, because she's a musical example of that elusive Clintonian ideal: a consensus builder. And a babe shall lead them.... —CHRIS WILLMAN/PHOTOGRAPH BY CLEO SULLIVAN

11

SUNDAY 15 JANUARY: *126 LBS, (EXCELLENT),* alcohol units 0, cigarettes 29 (*v.v. bad, esp. in 2 hours),* calories 3,879 (repulsive), negative thoughts 942 (approx. based on av. per minute), minutes spent counting negative thoughts, 127 (approx.) • On any given week, the best-seller list is a veritable boys' club. The usual suspects—Clancy, Grisham, Crichton, King, and, in 1998, Tom Wolfe—specialize in testosteronated prose: military-industrial intrigue, litigious villains, sci-fi high jinks, and exhaustive (and exhausting) sociopolitical girth. Given the hairy-chested competition, the phenomenal underdog success of Viking's *Bridget Jones's Diary* makes novelist Helen Fielding 1998's heaviest literary hitter. "For something that started comparably small," says John F. Baker, editorial director of *Publishers Weekly,* "it's gone pretty much through the roof." • If *Diary* were a movie (and by early 2000 it will be, courtesy of Working Title Films, makers of *Four Weddings and a Funeral*), Hollywood would call it a "chick flick." But while Fielding invented a persona that apparently resonates with the entire 20th-century female population, she's beguiled quite a few men as well, judging by the book's success: more than 3 million copies in print worldwide, 27 U.S. reprints, translations in 25 languages, availability in 33 countries. • It's hard to imagine a more likable poster girl for entertainment's new preoccupation: the neurotic single woman (think the various female *Friends,* Grace of NBC's *Will &,* not to mention Ally McBeal). But while Bridget may be self-obsessed and insecure ("...am fat, have spot on chin, and desire only to sit on cushion eating chocolate"), she's also intelligent, funny, and painfully real—a "spot-on" characterization, as the British would say. And the world did indeed start speaking Bridget's language: Her inventive lexicon—particularly *Singleton* (generic unattached female) and *Smug Marrieds* (self-satisfied couples, and there really aren't any other kind)—seemed to hijack our vocabulary like a hardcover *Austin Powers.* As *Four Weddings* screenwriter Richard Curtis told EW, "It's almost Dickensian how [the novel] has become part of our language." As one "Singleton" American fan said at a promo event for *Diary,* "This book is my friggin' life." So much for the fear that Bridget was too British. • Fielding's ingenious idea was to write a plot-driven novel organized in the chatty, abbreviated style of a diary; each entry begins with a few daily goals ("Wish to be like Tina Brown, though not, obviously, quite so hardworking") and an update on Bridget's unstable weight and love life ("I will not sulk about having no boyfriend, but develop inner poise and authority and sense of self as woman of substance...as best way to obtain boyfriend"). As some have pointed out, *Diary* is in fact a canny retelling of *Pride and Prejudice.* "Actually, I just stole the plot from *Pride and Prejudice,*" says Fielding, 40. "I thought it had been very well market-researched over a number of centuries." In truth, Fielding, now at work on the sequel—"We'll see what happens when someone like Bridget actually gets the guy"— developed Jones as an eponymous column for Britain's *The Independent.* A journalist and novelist (she's equally proud of her first book, *Cause Celeb,* a satire about charity workers in Africa, "only nobody bought that one"), Fielding is single and London-based, but, as she likes to point out to readers, she is *not* Bridget Jones. Still, international success has brought life alarmingly closer to art. "I've gone from being this rather frantically disorganized journalist to someone who gets to fly around the world," she says. "Now I'm always frantically fighting to turn up on time. So, I guess I'm more like Bridget every day." Considering that Fielding titled her first chapter "An Exceptionally Bad Start," things have turned out rather well. Or, as Bridget might say, "Hah! Excellent progress." —ANDREW ESSEX/PHOTOGRAPH BY VALERIE PHILLIPS

helen fielding

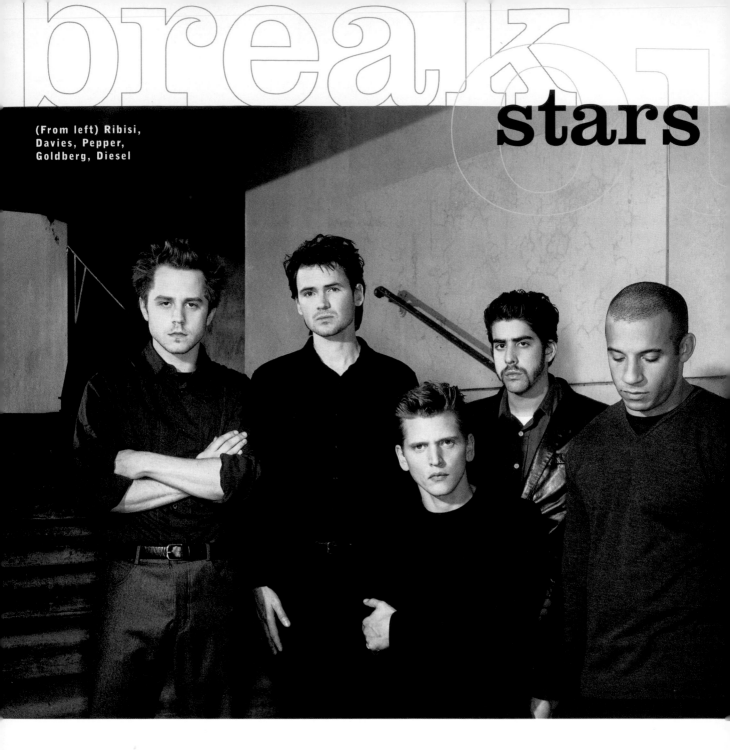

(From left) Ribisi, Davies, Pepper, Goldberg, Diesel

PRIVATE RYAN'S TROOPS > best new comrades-in-arms <

PLAYING SOLDIER WITH STUNNING VERISIMILITUDE—right down to the open-eyed death rattles—they burned themselves into the hearts and minds of audiences. Now casting agents have their radars fixed on the squad of four-star, dogfaced (okay, more like *puppy*-dog-faced) grunts of *Saving Private Ryan*. Among the actors' new assignments: a starring role as Pete in the film version of TV's *The Mod Squad* for Giovanni Ribisi, 23, who'd guested on *Friends* before Steven Spielberg drafted him as medic Wade. Barry Pepper, 28, *Ryan*'s Baptist rifleman, showed up on Will Smith's tail in *Enemy of the State*; he'll appear opposite Hanks again in *The Green Mile*, Stephen King's prison saga. The film's anguished coward, Jeremy Davies, 29, checked into Wim Wenders' *The Million Dollar Hotel*, opposite Mel Gibson. Vin Diesel, 31, wrapped the sci-fi thriller *Pitch Black* and plans to direct and star in *Doormen*. But postwar life seems busiest for Adam Goldberg, 28, *Ryan*'s Mellish. While looking for a distributor for his pre-G.I. writing-directing bow, *Scotch and Milk*, he jumped into *EdTV* for Ron Howard, portrayed a '70s record producer ("complete with dashiki and Afro") in *Sunset Strip*, and will shoot two TV pilots in 1999. "I'm finding I don't have to do actual auditions lately," says Goldberg. "I take meetings." In other words, the boot-camp thing is history. —STEVE DALY/PHOTOGRAPH BY DAN WINTERS

NATALIE IMBRUGLIA

> best new import <

NOT MUCH SECRECY to Natalie Imbruglia's success: Who among us doesn't hope to look that good feeling that bad? Others had recorded "Torn" before the 23-year-old Australian got to it (as the English press was fond of nagging), but she was the hitmaker-in-waiting whose confidently breathy reading so effectively prettified this anthem of emotional debasement and shame...and there's no shame in that. Nothing in the rest of the former TV actress' debut album, *Left of the Middle*, has quite the same urgency, and the career-artist-or-flash-in-the-pan debate continues to rage. Yet none of that mattered if you were a teenager in crisis. Courtney Love may have tried to put a melodic face on despondency in 1998, but Imbruglia was the cause's infinitely blue-eyed poster girl, and "Torn" the year's crucial bubblegum blues. —CHRIS WILLMAN

MASTER P

NEW ORLEANS-BASED RAP entrepreneur Master P (a.k.a. Percy Miller) has called himself a "ghetto Bill Gates," but maybe a homeboy Howard Stern is more like it. If P, 28, hasn't yet become the king of all media, it's not for lack of trying: In 1998, his independent No Limit Records landed hit albums from the likes of Snoop Dogg, Mia X, and C-Murder with clocklike regularity; he achieved his dream of a theatrically released motion picture, *I Got the Hook-Up*, thanks to Dimension Films; he's currently shooting hoops professionally with the Continental Basketball Association; *and* he has plans to produce a comedy show for cable. The workaholic keeps a close watch on his business—worth as much as $100 million—and vows he'll never go the way of Suge Knight and Death Row Records. "You've got to learn from others' [mistakes]," says P. "That's what you call soldier survival." Still, for all his talk of running No Limit "like corporate America," P's gangsta instincts remain; as he raps on one song, "Tupac and Biggie taught me a lesson/Never leave [home] without your Smith & Wesson." —TOM SINCLAIR/PHOTOGRAPH BY AMY GUIP

TAMARA JENKINS

FOR A WHILE THERE, it looked like every teenage girl on film would be narrowly escaping death at the hands of a slasher. Then along came *Slums of Beverly Hills*, a haunting and humorous paean to coming of age in the '70s from first-time writer-director Tamara Jenkins. Eliciting a career-defining performance from up-and-comer Natasha Lyonne, and a best-in-years performance from Marisa Tomei, Jenkins perfectly depicted the horrors of growing up poor and motherless in the country's poshest zip code (which she did), while also finding the undeniable humor in tube socks, shag carpets, and vibrators. "I was definitely handed this strange brew of a childhood," says Jenkins, 35, whose modest rewards from the movie include a bigger New York pad and a fax machine. Real validation, however, came from a childhood idol: After seeing *Slums*, "Gene Simmons gave me a Kiss rhinestone T-shirt and a copy of *Kisstory*," says Jenkins. "Let's face it, when Gene Simmons calls, you know you've made it." —JESSICA SHAW/PHOTOGRAPH BY ERIC JOHNSON

SEAN HAYES, MEGAN MULLALLY
best new sidekicks

FOR FANS OF *MONDAY NIGHT FOOTBALL* who've been missing *Will & Grace* (now moved to Tuesdays), here's a primer: The NBC sitcom is about the friendship between a gay man (lawyer Will) and a straight woman (interior decorator Grace), and while the family-values brigade has greeted the show with surprising silence, critics and viewers have gone crazy over its sidesplitting second fiddles. As Will's other best friend, Jack, Sean Hayes, 28, provides a smartly rendered flamboyance (his comic skills turn a gay male stereotype into a stitch); as Grace's rich-bitch assistant Karen, Megan Mullally, 40, steals scenes with a sneer. Put Hayes and Mullally together, and you have the most potent comic duo since Burns and Allen (or at least since Jerry and Elaine). "There's a flirtatious quality to their relationship," says Mullally, a Broadway musical vet. "I'm the diva he's always wanted to be." —JESS CAGLE/PHOTOGRAPH BY ART STREIBER

CHRIS TUCKER
> best new comic <

LIKE SOME MAD cross between Richard Pryor and Bugs Bunny on speed, Chris Tucker burst from the sidelines and into the national consciousness in 1998. Sure, the 26-year-old hyperkinetic comic has been hilarious for eons (check out his ghetto-stoner turn in 1995's *Friday* if you don't believe it), but the hugely popular *Rush Hour*—in which he swiped the spotlight from a dazed-but-game Jackie Chan—marked a crossover event of epic proportions. Zipping back and forth on the screen, firing jokes in his mosquito-pitched falsetto, he led the charge to an out-of-left-field box office take of $132 million and became a bona fide star in the process. Next up: a stadium stand-up pic à la *Richard Pryor Live on the Sunset Strip*—which should solve one recurring problem: "Every time I get a script I have to try and make it more, you know, me," says Tucker, who claims he's improvised most of his movie lines. As for his newfound megastardom, the kid dubbed "little Eddie Murphy" in high school says it's no surprise: "I know what's funny." Twenty-nine million *Rush Hour* fans would have to agree. —DANIEL FIERMAN/
PHOTOGRAPH BY CHRISTOPHER KOLK

DIXIE CHICKS > best new country band

WHEN IT COMES TO SETTING country-music records, the D Chicks spent 1998 making Garth Brooks look like a wheezing old n Their Monument Records debut, *Wide Open Spaces*, went double plati before the public could even ask the trio where it got its name. "From Little Feat song 'Dixie Chicken,'" says banjo-playing Emily Erwin. actually called ourselves that for a while, and taped rubber chickens to instruments to get attention, but it seemed silly, so we shortened the n to Chicks." Whatever the name, the act became the first to win the Cou Music Association's Horizon Award (for best rookie) *and* Group of the \ "It's overwhelming," says Erwin (right), 26, who's joined by her sister, dler Martie Seidel (left), 29, and lead singer Natalie Maines, 24. E and Seidel are hardly rookies, though; they did three albums with anc lead singer, which Erwin hopes "never surface," since "they don't have pure Dixie Chicks sound." Which is? "Old-time country played with a sensibility by three blonds is the best I can figure it." —KEN TUCKER

DOMINIQUE SWAIN > best new ingenue <

ADRIAN LYNE MAY NOT HAVE made good on his promise to best Stanley Kubrick, but his *Lolita* could at least lay claim to a better Lolita, in the long-legged form of Dominique Swain. The Malibu-bred teen instinctively understood the fine line between a child's conniving and the guile of a grown-up seductress. So while the filmmakers may have hemmed and hawed over whether to consider Nabokov's satire a tragic love story, Swain didn't buy any of it: "Humbert was a sicko for sure," she says. "I don't think it could have been at all romantic." The moments when a maturing Swain retreated from Jeremy Irons' embrace into a girly giggle were as chilling as any horror-movie scene, but also a funny blast of fresh air in Lyne's underoxygenated morality play. Next up, Swain may play a nymph of a different kind, a flower child, in *Summer of Love*. Let's hope she'll prove as dead-on at 18, playing 18, as she was at 15, playing 12 playing 28. —CW/PHOTOGRAPH BY ANDREW MACPHERSON

CATHERINE ZETA-JONES

> best new heartbreaker <

THE SWORD RESTS GENTLY against the fireplace in her new house in Pacific Palisades, but Catherine Zeta-Jones carries the mark of Zorro with her wherever she goes. And it can be quite a burden. After recognizing her in a bar as the woman who sliced and diced her way to Antonio Banderas' heart in *The Mask of Zorro*, a young man challenged Zeta-Jones, half jokingly, to a duel. "Try me again," she told him with a devilish smile, "and I'll cut your bits off." She was just as sharp with Bill Clinton; an invite to a White House party prompted a no-show. "I was too busy working," says the 28-year-old Zeta-Jones. "Besides, I don't find parties all that fascinating." Ever since the Welsh-born beauty had her dress Ginsu'd on screen, she's been cutting deals left and right. She's A-teaming it next with Sean Connery in *Entrapment* (she'll play an art thief), then with Liam Neeson in *The Haunting of Hill House*. The latter will find Zeta-Jones boasting psychic powers—somehow appropriate given her supernatural charms. —DAVID HOCHMAN/ PHOTOGRAPH BY ANDREW SOUTHAM

ANDREA BOCELLI
> best new voice <

HONEY, IT GETS LONELY out in the suburbs. There's the stupid job, that butt-numbing commute, those whining kids—and then there's Hubby over there, the man of your dreams, snoring in front of the tube before you've even had time to give the putz a back rub. Darn it, what ever happened to...(trill the *R* when you say it)...*romanza*?! But then you switch to PBS and hear the sweet, soaring tenor of this gorgeous blind Italian man, Andrea Bocelli. Okay, you think, here is a man who understands love! Here is a man whose arias and Tuscan street ballads can take me out of this humdrum routine, back to that place where the heart is more than a muscle under the rib cage! "Maybe in my voice there is something, I don't know," the 40-year-old Bocelli muses, wondering how his *Romanza* album became a platinum-selling Stateside sensation this year. "My secret is to sing with heart. Always. From the soul." Listen closely, Mr. Bocelli, and you'll hear a collective sigh.—JEFF GORDINIER/ PHOTOGRAPH BY DAVID BARRY

FELICITY HUFFMAN
> best new 'Sports' woman <

PLAYING PRODUCER Dana Whitaker on ABC's *Sports Night*, Felicity Huffman gives TV one of its most briskly efficient, emotionally vulnerable, and verbally cutting characters. Though mainly a Chicago-trained stage actress, Huffman, 36, has tangled with TV before. "I was supposed to have a recurring role in—what's that show about the guy who gets his paper delivered early? [*Early Edition*]—but that fell through. I was cast in *Thunder Alley* [an Ed Asner sitcom], but apparently I was about as funny as anthrax." Given how vital and cliché-free her single working woman is, she should now consider herself anthrax-immune. Coming up: TNT's *A Travesty*, written by her husband, actor William H. Macy (*ER*, *Fargo*), and director Paul Thomas Anderson's new film *Magnolia*. And she says her windy Windy City chum, David Mamet, is writing a role for her in his new play. Yikes: Isn't Dave kinda rough on the gals? "Am I the only person who thinks he writes very challenging roles for women?" she shoots back. *Sports* fans, start your engines! — KT/PHOTOGRAPH BY JEFFREY THURNHER

best of the best

THE X-FACTOR | EDWARD NORTON

EDWARD NORTON WAS RAISED in the planned community of Columbia, Md., a suburban model of tranquility, harmony, and order. Later he went to school at Yale, home of all that's cerebral. In 1998 he played two major roles, a jangly, manic gambler in *Rounders* and a murdering neo-Nazi skinhead in *American History X*, and was utterly, unnervingly convincing in each. If that's not acting, what is? "[What] I'm trying to achieve on a creative level," Norton explained, "are very distinct characters that you can get lost in without the inflection and interference of what you know about me." So pretend you don't know that stuff about Yale and the suburb, or that he's been good friends with Courtney Love, maybe very good friends. He may not think you appreciate the fact that there's not a better young actor working today. —JAMIE MALANOWSKI

GLORY DIAZ

WE KNEW THERE WAS something about Cameron. In 1997, she managed to outshine Julia Roberts as the sweet-as-peaches fiancée in *My Best Friend's Wedding*, memorably croaking out a karaoke version of "I Just Don't Know What to Do With Myself." But Hollywood knew what to do with Diaz: make her a star. "When we saw Cameron in *Wedding*, she had that glow that we needed," recalls Bobby Farrelly, half of the sibling duo that hatched Diaz's blockbuster, *There's Something About Mary*. Giving new meaning to the term *box office gross*, the 1998 hit comedy found a luminous Diaz driving a gaggle of grody guys to erotic distraction (can anyone say "bad hair day"?). "I read some of the scenes," Diaz said, "and I knew it was sick—but hilarious." In fact, the offbeat humor is right in step with Diaz's own style: Her next film, the very black comedy *Very Bad Things*, kept up her quirky streak. And that's just fine, because where Cameron goes, we'll follow. —JOE NEUMAIER/PHOTOGRAPH BY ANDREW SOUTHAM

GOLDEN GIRL

HEATHER GRAHAM

"I GUESS IT COULD be that Catholic-girl-goes-crazy type of thing," Heather Graham has said of the nexus between her straight-as-a-white-picket-fence upbringing and the unconventional roles she loves. Then again, maybe it's because "I like characters who are more out there or sexual, or independent movies that deal with different subject matter." Whatever the reason, Graham has become the new thinking man's It Girl, an indie-film fixture who first made a splash as the naive Nadine in *Drugstore Cowboy*, quickened pulses as the roller-skating nymph in *Boogie Nights* and almost got *Two Girls and a Guy* slapped with an NC-17 rating over her love scene with Robert Downey Jr. Graham has made occasional forays into mainstream Hollywood, such as *Lost in Space*. But that's not where her heart is: "I want to play characters who are more interesting than your typical Hollywood girlfriend," she has said. Graham typical? Not a chance. —NANCY SIDEWATER/ PHOTOGRAPH BY MOSHE BRAKHA

'HELLO' AGAIN

THIS WASN'T IN THE SCRIPT. The Beastie Boys, once the personification of snotty obnoxiousness, weren't supposed to grow up to be socially aware humanists talking about spirituality, helping to organize benefit concerts for the people of Tibet, and dropping rhymes like "The disrespect to women has got to be through." Yet Adam Horovitz (Adrock, left), Adam Yauch (MCA, center), and Mike Diamond (Mike D) have embraced adulthood with convincing grace, striving to do good while doing well, and continuing to grow artistically. Their multi-platinum album *Hello Nasty* was the most succulent slice of post-punk hip-hop electro-rock heard in 1998. For successfully juggling piety with a pie-in-the-eye ethos (no mean feat), these fellas were our Boys to Men of the Year. —TOM SINCLAIR

JUST SO YOU KNOW, there were no catfights on the set of *Stepmom* except—*gasp!*—when the cameras were rolling. "If you make a movie with a male star," asserted Susan Sarandon, who plays a divorced mother of two stricken with a life-threatening illness, "everyone assumes you're f---ing. If it's a female star, everyone assumes you're fighting." But the only tongues set wagging this time out have been those of Academy voters, as both actresses shone in ways we haven't seen before. For Roberts, who plays the young woman who tries to fill Sarandon's shoes, it was a green light to venture beyond the chipper chippies we're used to. As for Sarandon, the film was an opportunity to take her bitchy side out for a joyride. The sparks *did* fly when these two magnetic women went toe-to-toe—and they lit up the screen. —MARC BERNARDIN/PHOTOGRAPH BY MATTHEW ROLSTON

FACE TIME | CONAN O'BRIEN

IT SEEMS, FINALLY, THAT HIS TIME HAS ARRIVED. Once the Rodney Dangerfield of late-night comics (translation: He got no respect), Conan O'Brien emerged in 1998 as the Talk-Show Host of Choice among Gen-Xers. And it doesn't take a Harvard grad (like O'Brien) to see why: The 35-year-old ex–*SNL* and –*Simpsons* writer with the face of an altar boy and the sensibility of a fraternity prankster struck a chord with viewers (some 2.6 million a night) with his mix of blissful silliness and pointed irreverence. Harkening back to the chatty, skit-heavy style of Johnny Carson, Conan & Co. have brought us such characters as the Shirtless Moron and the Masturbating Bear, all the while seeming to have a gas (often literally). "Sometimes I worry about the show," Conan has said, "and then I think, It's 12:30 at night, for God's sake.... If you have any complaints, you shouldn't be up that late anyway." —PHOTOGRAPH BY RICHARD MCLAREN

ACTUALLY, SHE'S BEEN FAKING IT all along. Ever since her breakthrough moment—feigning orgasm in 1989's *When Harry Met Sally*—Ryan has reigned as the queen of romantic comedy, but she has said: "I am just not a romantic.... I am not a sentimental person." Trouble is, no one believes her. Which is why Ryan had such a heavenly year: first, starring in *City of Angels* as a cardiac surgeon who melts the heart of winged hunk Nicolas Cage, then falling in love online with her *Sleepless in Seattle* buddy Tom Hanks in Nora Ephron's feel-good flick *You've Got Mail*. So if she's so unmushy, what keeps bringing Ryan back to her warm, fuzzy roots? "What's funny to do in romantic comedy is hate-and-love," she has said. "All that great antagonism is really fun." Sounds like she's found a surefire formula for staying close to our hearts. —MATTHEW MCCANN FENTON

SHAPE-SHIFTER

BUSTA RHYMES

BUSTA RHYMES JUST WON'T STAND STILL. It's not only a matter of his manic stage presence or motormouthed rapping style—the man's mind moves as fast as the frenetically paced video for his hit song "Dangerous." Give him half a chance, and he'll expound on race, politics, and religion for hours, giving the lie to those who view him as merely the clown prince of rap. Just as he does with his dreadlocks, Rhymes—who has described himself as "dominant, aggressive, and moody"—twists his persona into an endless variety of shapes: by turns comic, tender, vicious, and madcap. His abiding interest in all things apocalyptic is evident in the title of his just-released third solo album, *E.L.E. (The Final World Front)*, certainly one of 1998's most explosive hip-hop records. As the millennium approaches, expect this mercurial rapper to keep blowing up. —TOM SINCLAIR/PHOTOGRAPH BY DANNY CLINCH

FANNY GIRL

JENNIFER LOPEZ

SHE'S BEEN *MUY CALIENTE* since her days at *In Living Color*. But this onetime Fly Girl flew higher and faster in 1998 than anyone could have imagined. Anyone, that is, but Lopez herself. She's "at an all-time high of tornado-whirlwind-storm right now," Lopez says. And it's not hard to see why: Her love life keeps gossip columnists working overtime (she's been linked with everyone from rapper Sean "Puffy" Combs to boxer Oscar De La Hoya); her relentlessly vertical career trajectory has made her the highest-paid Latina actress ever ($2 million for 1998's *Out of Sight*); and—let's face it—she's got a bum so, well, *out there* that it's been a joke on *Hollywood Squares* ("I could serve coffee using my rear as a ledge"). So what's next? A new CD that may finally make Lopez the kind of star she's always wanted to be. "People like Cher and Bette Midler and Diana Ross and Barbra Streisand—that's always been the kind of career I'd hoped to have," she explains. "I want it all." —MARC BERNARDIN/PHOTO-GRAPH BY RUVEN AFANADOR

APPLAUSE

STRAIGHT MAN | **JIM CARREY**

"JIMMY'S NOT A HAM," HIS FATHER ONCE SAID. "He's the whole pig." Whichever way you slice it, the no-holds-barred comic proved in 1998 that he wasn't just another silly face. As the only member of *The Truman Show* who's not in on the joke, Carrey gave his most ambitious performance to date, earning buckets of serious critical acclaim and—somebody stop him!—even Oscar talk. "It's not Shakespeare, but it's a more human character than anything I've done," concedes the actor, who'll next morph into the late funnyman Andy Kaufman in Milos Forman's biopic *Man on the Moon*. "You have to be able to put away the mask of mirth at times," Carrey has said of what led him to the role. So how much of this "true man" surrounded by fakers does Carrey see in himself? "Basically, I'm a lot like Truman. I'm the sort of guy who wants to make everybody happy." —NANCY SIDEWATER/PHOTOGRAPH BY ROBERT TRACHTENBERG

PSYCHO MAN | VINCE VAUGHN

WHEN HE WALKS INTO BARS, Vince Vaughn gets the same response his character Trent gave to his would-be hipster friends in *Swingers*: "You are so *money!*" But in his case, money talks. After starring as a loser lothario in the 1996 film, the Illinois-bred Vaughn played equally selfish—or downright scary—characters in *The Lost World*, *Return to Paradise*, and *Clay Pigeons*. But as mother-lovin' man-boy motelier Norman Bates in Gus Van Sant's controversial remake of *Psycho*, Vaughn reinvented a role already enshrined in film history by Anthony Perkins. "I figured I would just go in with my own interpretation and not try to mimic him," says the 28-year-old Vaughn. Does he fret about adding another lady-killer to his résumé? "I never really worried about being liked in movies," he has said. Maybe not in movies, but in real life? You're *money*, baby.

—JOE NEUMAIER/PHOTOGRAPH BY ROBERT MAXWELL

DÉJÀ BLUE

SEAN LENNON

THE LOOK WASN'T A SURPRISE—like his half brother, Julian, 23-year-old Sean Lennon has his father John's moonfaced impishness and low-voltage cool. No, what caught everyone's attention was, interestingly, the music. *Into the Sun*, boasting a double meaning in its title, had what John would have called instant karma. Even Gen-Xers who think of Beatles music as filler for sneaker commercials recognized Sean's genetic gifts: emotional authenticity and a knack for experimentation. The singer-guitarist, only 5 when his father was murdered, inherited more than just good genes: "The first music I listened to was on my dad's jukebox," he recalls. So *Sun* managed to be that rare thing—a first record by an edgy young musician with a sense of history. —JOE NEUMAIER/ PHOTOGRAPH BY ANTON CORBIJN

RAPSCALLIONS AT LARGE | **WAKING NED DEVINE**

MOVIES ABOUT IRELAND tend to fall into two categories: the Northern, in which the films are inhabited by hard men and offer grim, bleak, unflinching looks at the Troubles, and the Southern, in which we find the human equivalents of leprechauns and faeries gamboling about, the atmosphere and the events verge on magical, and folks are twinkly and romantic and cute. Firmly entrenched in the latter category is the feather light *Waking Ned Devine*—a caper movie of sorts in which a village full of as quaint a group of folks as ever kissed the Blarney stone (led by Ian Bannen and David Kelly, the charmers pictured below) scheme to milk the government of the lottery winnings of a man who died of shock when his number was picked. And when all the counting's done, Fox Searchlight hopes to find a *Full Monty*-size pot of gold at the end of the rainbow. —JAMIE MALANOWSKI/PHOTOGRAPH BY ETHAN HILL

EASY DERIDER

DAVID SPADE

IF ONE FAMOUS TV character could turn the world on with a smile, then David Spade can put it down with a sneer. It was his expression of choice on *SNL* and he brought it with him to NBC's *Just Shoot Me*. A good thing, too: As magazine employee Dennis Finch, Spade dishes out snide asides—"Wait, I just remembered, you're boring and my legs work"—that personify late-'90s ironic hip. Though it lost the battle for *Seinfeld*'s 9 p.m. slot, his show inherited something even better: the fab four's all-for-me-and-*can-you-all-shut-up* attitude. "A couple years down the line, I'll be cockier," says Spade. "I'll have a karate instructor on the set—[they'll] call me Hong Kong Finchy." Then his fists may fly as fast as his insults. —JOE NEUMAIER/ PHOTOGRAPH BY SAM JONES

FUNNY FACE | **DON KNOTTS**

IF YOU NEVER THOUGHT THE MEEK would inherit the earth, you haven't seen Barney Fife bug his eyes out in frustration or Ralph Furley bluster up a storm. Which is to say, you haven't seen the comic genius of Don Knotts. After winning fans (and five Emmys) in the '60s as the perpetually addled Deputy Fife on *The Andy Griffith Show*, Knotts in 1979 traded in his badge for a floral ascot to play swingin' oldster Furley on *Three's Company*. In 1998 he was back, as the embodiment of retro chic in *Pleasantville*, a mystical TV repairman who helps zap two teens into a blissfully bland black-and-white sitcom. "It's a good feeling to have endured," he has said, "but, golly, all I really did was stick around." Long enough to witness a full-scale pop-culture embrace, with one of his early films, *The Incredible Mr. Limpet*, being updated for *today's* clown prince, Jim Carrey. If looking at Knotts calls to mind a pair of rabbit-ear antennae with legs, do not adjust your set: He's *still* the funniest thing around. —JOE NEUMAIER/PHOTOGRAPH BY ETHAN HILL

THE HEIRESS

NATASHA RICHARDSON

SHE HASN'T HAD the early luck of her mother, the luck to emerge from *Blow-Up* as the poster girl for cool sexuality or to command the screen as *Mary, Queen of Scots*. No, it's fallen to Natasha Richardson—radiant, soulful, swan-necked—to give a series of canny performances in flawed films, so that most people know little more about her than her pedigree as one of the performing Redgraves and her marriage to Liam Neeson. But 1998 stood as a breakthrough year, when Richardson so smashingly starred in *Cabaret* on Broadway (winning a Tony as the in-over-her-head Sally Bowles, who takes her walk on the wild side as the night of Nazism descends) and then followed up by playing the fetching mom in a frothy remake of *The Parent Trap*. A successful year, but one she frames with a levelheadedness learned at the kitchen table. "I'm ambitious in terms of how I push myself, but not for a huge, No. 1 box office hit," she has said. "I just want to do good parts." —JAMIE MALANOWSKI/PHOTOGRAPH BY NORMAN JEAN ROY

the **year** in review

LADIES AND GENTS, welcome to 1998: a year when Norman Bates returned to the front desk, wearing his traditional granny wig and dress, Private Ryan returned to Normandy, wearing the tourist's traditional beige zippered windbreaker and sporty slacks, and even Zorro returned, wearing the traditional black ensemble with cape. A year when TV execs, responding swiftly to the incarceration of the *Seinfeld* Four, the departure of Larry Sanders, and the death of Det. Bobby Simone, designated *Dawson's Creek* as the center of the known universe. A year when size mattered more for some (that sinking ship raked in $600 million and took home 11 Oscars) than for others (that mutant lizard smashed a lot of buildings but, alas, no box office records). A year of near misses (a publicity-friendly asteroid) and even a near Mrs. (Dennis Rodman, *what* were you thinking?). A year when styles got jiggy, with back lines plunging *down to there* and pregnant fashion plates showing *out to here*. And finally, a year of spooky synchronicity: Who'd have thought that life, in the form of Monica Lewinsky and surprise bomb attacks, could so closely imitate art, in the form of *Primary Colors* and *Wag the Dog*? But that was the news from 1998. Good night, and have a pleasant 1999.

> I don't care if we were nominated for Best Morons, because I'd think, Well, I got nominated with [best friend] Ben [Affleck], and that's pretty cool. If you put us together, you might actually make a whole, creative, interesting individual. We're a lot like the Wonder Twins. —**MATT DAMON,** *on the thrill of being nominated for a screenwriting Oscar for* Good Will Hunting

THE YEAR IN REVIEW

orders from NBC West Coast president **Don Ohlmeyer**, who did not find Macdonald "funny" (unlike Ohlmeyer's name, which, when uttered by **David Letterman** with the word *idiot* during a Macdonald appearance on *Late Show* Jan. 7, sent audiences into paroxysms of laughter). Ohlmeyer seemingly got the last laugh during the NBA Finals, when he decreed that NBC would turn down ads for Macdonald's movie *Dirty Work*; his decision was later reversed. Also, a year after making headlines for a hotel-room tryst with a woman other than **Kathie Lee**, **Frank Gifford** is dropped, after 27 years, as anchor on ABC's *Monday Night Football* and replaced by ex-quarterback **Boomer Esiason**.

> PEOPLE CAN WEAR THEM WHEN THEY GO OUT FOR A ROW THROUGH THE DEAD
The **J. Peterman Company** catalog, known for its highish prices, purple-prosed item descriptions, and connection to *Seinfeld*, makes a splash by selling out almost its entire inventory of costumes and props from the film *Titanic*, including lifeboats priced at $25,000 each.

> HE'D BEEN WAITING TO GET A WORD IN EDGEWISE
Thirty-five years after the suicide of his first wife, American poet **Sylvia Plath**, and eight months before his own death from cancer, British poet laureate **Ted Hughes**—one of a very few laureates best known as someone's husband—finally tells his side of the story in *Birthday*

> HOPE SOMEBODY AT LEAST BOUGHT JERRY DINNER
With **Jerry Seinfeld** announcing the end of his series, NBC acts swiftly to lock up its remaining assets, giving **Jay Leno** a reported $75 million contract to keep him behind the *Tonight Show* desk until 2003 and paying Warner Bros. Television $13 million per episode for *ER*, the most ever spent for a TV series.

> OUSTED!
Norm Macdonald is axed from *Saturday Night Live*'s "Weekend Update" on

Big Mac attacked

NEVER START A BEEF WITH OPRAH Oprah Winfrey leaves the Amarillo courthouse after winning a multimillion-dollar defamation suit brought against her by Texas cattlemen (an appeal is pending). The Texans had had a cow when the "most powerful woman in entertainment" proclaimed her dismay about mad-cow disease during a 1996 episode: "It has just stopped me cold from eating another burger."

Letters. The book of poems, which portrays the lovers as almost helplessly doomed to their fates, goes into a second printing even before hitting bookstores.

> HEY NOW!
Soon after confirming that he expects to leave HBO's *The Larry Sanders Show* at the end of the season, **Garry Shandling** sues ex-manager **Brad Grey** of Brillstein-Grey Enterprises, claiming Grey entered into a conflict of interest by using his position as the comedian's manager to cut a series of

lucrative TV-production deals. The case is slated to go to trial in June 1999.

> RAGING BULL
Robert De Niro is detained for nine hours as French investigators question him about an international prostitution ring. Leaving the courthouse, De Niro shines a flashlight into paparazzi cameras in a vain attempt to ruin their pictures. He is later quoted as saying, "I am never going back to France. I'm going to tell my friends not to come, either. And I am going to send back my Legion of Honor medal."

> A FINELY AGED WHINE
Christina Crawford, 59, says she is personally reissuing *Mommie Dearest,* her account of her upbringing by **Joan Crawford,** "as I intended to publish it the

first time." The 20th-anniversary trade-paperback edition restores more than 100 pages that William Morrow axed from the original manuscript, much of it having to do with Joan and Christina's relationship as adults.

> IN A NAKED LUNGE TO SEEM INTERESTING...
Vice President **Al Gore** brags that former Harvard classmate **Erich Segal** based *Love Story*'s star-crossed Oliver Barrett IV and Jenny Cavilleri on himself and Tipper. The author politely begs to differ.

> HE IS, HOWEVER, STILL PERMITTED TO HANG OUT AT STARBUCKS
DC Comics decides to abandon its effort to hipify **Superman** with long hair and a new capeless wardrobe. The 11-month experiment, which began after a battle with "giant evil creatures," comes to an end as DC has the hero go back to his short hair and traditional costume.

> PEERING INTO THE GREAT MINDS OF OUR ERA...
Craig Kilborn of *The Daily Show* is quoted in *Esquire* as saying that head writer Lizz Winstead would perform a sexual act "if I wanted her to." He's suspended, she quits.

De Niro does his bit to discourage the Parisian paparazzi

> WHY DIDN'T THEY SEE IT COMING?

The parent company behind the once–**Dionne Warwick**-endorsed **Psychic Friends Network** files for bankruptcy protection. **Inphomation Communications Inc.** cited the high cost of infomercials and competition from other psychic phone lines that offer free 10-minute consultations.

THE YEAR IN REVIEW

> "OK FOR FIRST EFFORT; PLS MAKE MOODIER"

Stephen King's script for an *X-Files* episode is sent back by creator **Chris Carter** with instructions for revisions; it ultimately goes through multiple drafts before being broadcast.

> "I GET LOCKED UP, BUT I SHOPLIFT AGAIN..."

In the same month that **U2** promoters distribute 150,000 free condoms at Brazilian concerts, **Chumbawamba**'s Alice Nutter tells fans on *Politically Incorrect* to go out and steal the band's albums from record stores. (Virgin Megastores temporarily opt to put them behind the counter.)

> SATURDAY'S DWIGHT'S ALL RIGHT FOR KNIGHTING

Elton John (born Reginald Dwight), author of such song classics as "The Bitch Is Back," is named a Knight of the British Empire by England's **Queen Elizabeth**. "My joy at now receiving this great new honor is immeasurable," he says.

> THE PAMELA AND TOMMY WATCH

Not a good time for the video-age couple: A second sexually explicit **Pamela Anderson Lee** tape surfaces on the Internet, this one starring her and ex-beau (and Poison lead singer) **Bret Michaels**; **Tommy Lee** pleads no contest to one count of misdemeanor battery for assaulting a photographer and is ordered by an L.A. judge to undergo "anger-management" therapy as part of his sentence; and the pièce de résistance: Pamela lands on Mr. Blackwell's Worst-Dressed List.

> THAT'S THE POWER OF LOVE

Documentarian **Nick Broomfield**'s controversial *Kurt and Courtney* is yanked from the Sundance Film Festival because of legal threats from EMI Music Publishing, warning against the use of unlicensed music from Nirvana and Hole. (**Kurt Cobain**'s widow, **Courtney Love**, wasn't too thrilled with the film either.)

Broomfield's film was cut at Sundance

Still, it shows at San Francisco's Roxie Cinema, Feb. 27.

> "AND NOW, FROM THE THERAPEUTIC WHITE HOUSE..."

As the **Monica Lewinsky** story breaks, country singer **Naomi Judd** offers to pay for **President Clinton** to be treated at the Sierra Tucson sexual addiction clinic.

> SURPRISINGLY, 'PLAYGIRL' HAS YET TO GET IN TOUCH

During a February taping of the *American Comedy Awards*, *NewsRadio* cut-up **Andy Dick** is set to do a gag where he'd tear off his clothes and dance in a diaper with the computer-animated baby from *Ally McBeal*, but Dick "accidentally" drops both pants and diaper. Says Dick: "I fully apologize to anyone who had to look at my body."

> GETTING IN TOUCH WITH HIS INNER MONOPOLIST

In what may have been an effort to humanize his less-than-cuddly public image, Microsoft chairman/CEO (and richest guy in the history of the world) **Bill Gates** sings "Twinkle, Twinkle, Little Star" to Barbara Walters during an interview special. The Justice Department, appar-

GLOBE THEATER Jack Lemmon now has four Golden Globes in his trophy case, three of which he actually won. The fourth was given to him by Ving Rhames, who won a Globe for *Don King: Only in America*, but tearfully called Lemmon to the stage at the Jan. 18 ceremony, insisting his performance in *12 Angry Men* deserved the honor.

> Katie [Holmes] learned a new word from the makeup person: fellatio. Eighteen years of Catholic schools down the toilet after three weeks on *Dawson's Creek*. —JOSHUA JACKSON *on the adult language of his new teen drama*

ently unmoved, files an antitrust suit against Microsoft four months later.

> HOME IS WHERE THE, UH, YOU KNOW, IS

Former castratee/porn-star manqué **John Wayne Bobbitt** is hired at the Moonlight Bunny Ranch bordello, outside Carson City, Nev. Bobbitt says troubles finding employment led him to take the $50,000-a-year job. He claims what he really wants is to reunite with ex-wife (and castrator) Lorena.

> FAMILY MATTERS

Prime Suspect's Emmy-winning lead, **Helen Mirren**, weds director **Taylor Hackford**; **Hugh Hefner** and his second wife, ex–Playmate

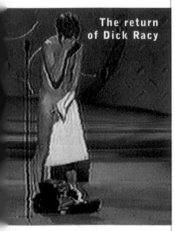

The return of Dick Racy

of the Year Kimberly Conrad Hefner, announce their separation on Jan. 20; **Minnie Driver** and *Good Will Hunting* costar

Matt Damon split—very publicly; **Sharon Stone** weds buff San Francisco newspaper editor **Phil Bronstein** on Feb. 14; **Woody Harrelson** marries longtime gal pal Laura Louie on Jan. 11; **Yanni**, New Age musician, and ex–*Dynasty* star **Linda Evans** announce they're splitting after nine years—though they expect their "friendship will always endure"; **Roseanne** files for divorce from third husband Ben Thomas on Jan. 8.

> TRIALS AND TRIBULATIONS

Daniel Baldwin, 37, is arrested for possession of cocaine on Feb. 3 in New York. He pleads guilty to disorderly conduct; **Robert Downey Jr.**, serving 114 days of a six-month sentence in L.A.'s Twin Towers jail complex for drug violations, is involved in a fight with another inmate; **Christian Slater** checks into jail for a three-month sentence after pleading guilty to striking his girlfriend and a police officer and being under the influence of a controlled substance; two photographers are convicted of false imprisonment after boxing in **Maria Shriver** and **Arnold Schwarzenegger**'s Mercedes twice on the way to their child's preschool. They are later sentenced to 60 and 90 days in jail; **Toni Braxton**, 29, files for bankruptcy on Jan. 23.

SOY VEY While Bob Dylan sang "Love Sick" at the Grammys, Michael Portnoy rushed the stage and writhed spastically until being removed (above). As Shawn Colvin (right, with cowinner John Leventhal) was accepting a songwriting Grammy for "Sunny Came Home," the Wu-Tang Clan's Ol' Dirty Bastard (who had just lost to Puff Daddy for Best Rap Album) also made an unexpected appearance on stage before being escorted off (below).

Some people only think about how they can make millions and millions of dollars, but I'm not looking at the movie for its commercial potential. To me, it's a question of artistic realization. Of answering the question that made the [Lost in Space] series so interesting. Whether or not hetero-androgynous relationships can absorb and accept and tolerate critical situations and eke out a solution. That's what intrigues me." —*LOST IN SPACE* **STAR WILLIAM HURT,** *who had nothing to worry about: The film was not the blockbuster others had expected*

THE YEAR IN REVIEW

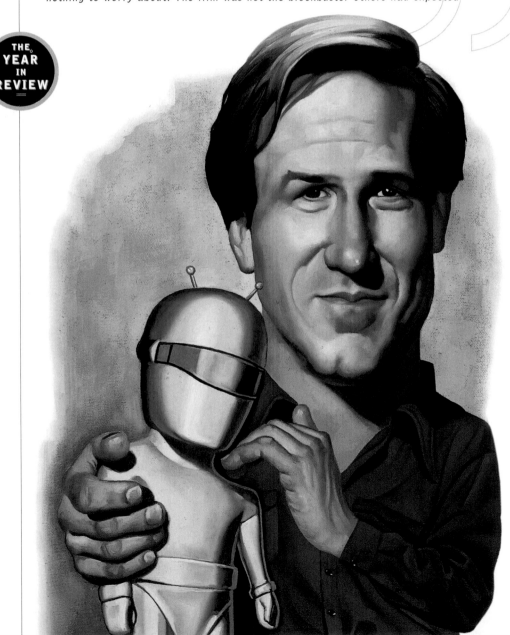

> **AND THE BEAT GOES ON...**
Mary Bono defeats *Waltons* pappy Ralph Waite to finish her late husband Sonny's term in Congress. By the impeachment hearings in October, she has gone from blonde to brunette and reportedly has begun dating again.

> **SLIP SLIDIN' AWAY**
After seven years of development and a reported $11 million investment, Paul Simon's coolly reviewed Broadway musical, *The Capeman*, closes after 127 performances.

> **HOW THE HECK DID THAT HAPPEN?**
Jodie Foster discloses that she is pregnant, but coyly refuses to disclose by whom, or "by what method."

> **IT'S TOO FAR AWAY TO CAUSE US DAMAGE, BUT IT MIGHT BE CLOSE ENOUGH TO OPEN A PLANET HOLLYWOOD ON**
A news report that a mile-wide asteroid will pass uncomfortably close to Earth in the year 2028 is thought to be bad news for Earth but an excellent publicity opportunity for the upcoming summer movies *Deep Impact* and *Armageddon*. The reports note that "close" in this case means 600,000 miles away.

> **HOW ABOUT A VOWEL FOR A HUNDRED MILLION?**
Garth Brooks and rap star Warren G settle a suit allowing them both to use the letter *g* as a logo. The rapper had been using it for several

years when Brooks decided that none of the 25 other letters in the alphabet quite captured his essence. At stake were millions of merchandising dollars.

> IF THE BANANA SPLITS, YOU MUST CONVICT

While **Fred Goldman**, one of the dads in the **O.J. Simpson** trial, gets his own TV special (called *Search for Justice*) on UPN, Simpson gives a BBC interview to journalist **Ruby Wax** in which he brags about all the women in his life and stages a fake stabbing with a banana.

O.J. takes a stab at things

> LOLLAPA-LOSER

Lollapalooza, the seven-year-old alternative music tour, is called off for the summer because of a lack of interest.

> ...WHO PROMPTLY CHUCKED IT INTO THE NORTH ATLANTIC

A heart-shaped diamond-encrusted sapphire made famous by **Kate Winslet** in *Titanic* is auctioned to an anonymous buyer for $2.2 million.

> OKAY, BUT IF HER NEXT SINGLE IS TITLED "WHIRLPOOL," WE'LL HAVE SOME QUESTIONS

As her *Ray of Light* album debuts at No. 2, **Madonna** is again mired in controversy: This time Magnetic Poetry owner Dave Kapell maintains that 47 of the 51 words used in Madonna's song "Candy Perfume Girl" also appear in the Magnetic Poetry Sequel game (those words that stick to refrigerator doors). The four that are original to the song: wish, rush, nerve, steam. Madonna's publicist claims that it is mere coincidence, and that she has never heard of Magnetic Poetry.

> WE SALUTE YOU, CAPTAIN TUTTLE!

After celebrating the second book from **David Bowie**'s new publishing venture—**William Boyd**'s "biography" of little-known Abstract Expressionist painter Nat Tate, who committed suicide at 31—Bowie and Boyd

LEAVE IT TO DIVAS "I've never considered myself a diva," demurred Gloria Estefan (shown at left, alongside Mariah Carey, Aretha Franklin, Carole King, Celine Dion, and Shania Twain), who donned a shiny, formfitting dress and perilously spikey high heels for VH1's *Divas Live* on April 14. "But I'm getting teased about it a lot now." The show, ostensibly held to benefit musical education in public schools (although the real draw was to see whether these women could survive an evening sharing one stage), became the highest-rated program in VH1's history and spawned an album on Epic Records.

WHO'DA THUNK IT? Mere days after being caught by an undercover police officer performing a lewd act at a public convenience in Beverly Hills (and how many of them could there be?), George Michael comes out of the closet on CNN. Asked why he is outing himself now, Michael says, "I've already kind of done that, haven't I?"

in which the tycoon's trophy wife and her boyfriend are prime suspects.

> BY COMPARISON, HANOI SEEMED COSMOPOLITAN...
Jane Fonda annoys her fellow Georgians by likening her adopted state to a Third World country. She apologizes.

> GOSH, YOU THINK YOU FINALLY FIND A SPOT THAT'S SAFE FROM LAWYERS...
Yves Montand's remains are exhumed to settle a nine-year-old paternity suit. DNA testing ultimately proves he is *not* the father of Aurore Drossart.

> THE REAL TRICK WOULD BE TO GET PEOPLE TO COME TO A RE-RELEASE OF 'GREASE 2'
Grease celebrates its 20th anniversary with a re-release, which makes $12.7 million its first weekend.

> HELL HATH NO FURY LIKE A WOMAN PORNED
"I love the Internet," Melrose Place actress **Alyssa Milano** says. "I just want to clean it up a bit." To that end,

Milano—whose mother tracks celebrity-porn images on the Web—sues five adult websites that are featuring unauthorized nude photos of her. Milano wins one suit and settles two out of court; the others are still pending.

> LUCKY HE STUCK AROUND TO TAKE ON GODZILLA
Hispanic rights activists urge Taco Bell to drop **Gidget**, a dog who says "Yo quiero Taco Bell" ("I want Taco Bell"), from its commercials; they contend the ads demean Spanish-speaking Americans. The spots continue to run.

> IN THE FOOT-STEPS OF MARLON BRANDO AND BRIGITTE BARDOT...
Drew Carey protests California's ban on restaurant smoking by lighting up at Barney's Beanery in front of a crowd of reporters.

> THE LEO WATCH
Leonardo DiCaprio files suit against *Playgirl* to stop it from printing nude photos of him. After a settlement is reached, pictures run; editor Ceslie Armstrong says she is fired after threatening to resign in protest over publication

reveal a hoax: The painter actually never existed. This later leaves many of the guests at the launch party, who had gone on about the important role of the nonexistent dead man in art history, a tad embarrassed.

> AND HE DIDN'T EVEN STAR IN 'BRAVEHEART'
Sean Connery is passed over for knighthood, arguably because of his support for the Scottish Nationalist Party, which favors independence from Britain.

> THIS MAN COULD GET BETTER CAREER ADVICE FROM AN EIGHT BALL
Christopher Darden, who became famous as one of the prosecutors in the **O.J. Simpson** trial, stars in the ABC TV-movie *Crimes of Passion* as a detective investigating the murder of a high-profile sports tycoon,

¡Yo Quiero Taco Bell!

> You know who appears by far the most in Englishmen's erotic dreams? The Queen. And she's no babe.
> —*PRIMARY COLORS* DIRECTOR **MIKE NICHOLS,** *trying to explain "our unconscious sexual connection to our leaders"*

Can y 'offer in Spa

of the photos: "It's an invasion of privacy; I can't be associated with it."

> THE PAMELA AND TOMMY WATCH

Tommy Lee pleads no contest to felony spousal abuse April 7 after a February incident in which he kicked **Pamela** as she held their son (within days, she filed for divorce).

> FAMILY MATTERS

Mariah Carey ends her five-year marriage to Sony mogul **Tommy Mottola** in the Dominican Republic, March 5; **Paula Abdul** files for divorce from clothing manufacturer Brad Beckerman, March 9; **Mira Sorvino** and **Quentin Tarantino** break up; **Rupert Murdoch** and his wife, Anna, separate, March 2; **Jennifer Aniston** and her occasional *Friends* costar **Tate Donovan** call it quits. She later takes up with **Brad Pitt**; **Robert De Niro** and wife Grace Hightower have their first child, March 18; **Puff Daddy** and his girlfriend, model Kim Porter, welcome a baby boy, April 1; **Michael Jackson** and his wife, Debbie Rowe, welcome a daughter on April 3.

> TRIALS AND TRIBULATIONS

Ex-con Jonathan Norman is found guilty of stalking **Steven Spielberg**, March 4; **Christian Slater** is released from jail March 14 after serving 60 days of a 90-day sentence (jailers say that Leonard Nimoy and Mike Myers were visitors); **Robert Downey Jr.** also gets out of the slammer, on March 31, after serving 113 days of a 180-day sentence for violating probation; an ex-nanny files suit against **Demi Moore** and **Bruce Willis,** alleging she was "shamelessly exploited and abused." The case is still pending.

KINGS (AND QUEENS) OF THE WORLD

Director James Cameron exults over one of *Titanic*'s 11 Oscars (1); Kim Basinger hugs her *L.A. Confidential* Supporting Actress trophy and hubby Alec Baldwin (2); it was *As Good as It Gets* for Best Actress Helen Hunt and Best Actor Jack Nicholson (3); Bart the Bear presents the Sound Effects Editing award; and four-time nominee Robin Williams finally wins—as Best Supporting Actor in *Good Will Hunting*.

may | june

Huddled in some New York hotel room drinking out of little bottles. —**WAYNE KNIGHT**, *a.k.a. Newman, on where he expected to be during the final episode of* Seinfeld

Heston brands Streisand "the Hanoi Jane of the Second Amendment," proving that even the best of actors need writers.

>BUT GET A LOAD OF THIS: NO 'SHOWGIRLS'

AFI releases its list of the 100 greatest films in the first 100 years of American cinema. *Citizen Kane* ranks No. 1.

>LOOK FOR ERIC'S NEXT SINGLE, FEATURING THE LYRIC "GONNA GET MY LAWYERS TO NULLIFY OUR PRENUP, BABY, AND GET YOU BARRED FROM THE SUMMER HOUSE"

Objecting to "Sick and Tired," a track on **Eric Clapton**'s *Pilgrim* album that features the lyric "I may have to blow your brains out, baby/Then you won't bother me no more," domestic-abuse awareness activists call upon Reprise to change the words to this "hate message to women" and donate proceeds to violence-prevention programs. Reprise declines.

>CALL IT THE PUBLIC'S RIGHT TO NOT KNOW

The California Supreme Court decides that producers

>MAYBE THEY SHOULD SETTLE THIS WITH A WINNER-TAKE-ALL ROUND OF PAINTBALL

Hollywood liberal **Barbra Streisand** and NRA frontman **Charlton Heston** exchange verbal volleys over a TV docudrama she executive-produced, *The Long Island Incident, Based on the True Story of Carolyn McCarthy*, about the woman who ran for Congress on an anti-gun platform after her husband died in a 1993 commuter-train massacre.

Harrison Ford doe[...] his act on *Mag[...]*

NBC WANTS TO HOLD A REUNION SPECIAL THE INSTANT THEY GET OUT *Seinfeld* signs off. Between Jerry's announcement on Dec. 24, 1997, that he is leaving and the last broadcast May 14, the show benefits from dozens of magazine covers and hundreds of news stories. The final episode is seen by an estimated 133.9 million people, prompts farewell parties across the land, and is widely judged as anticlimactic. The series ends on an edgy, unsentimental note, with the four leads in jail.

of reality programming can be held liable for invading people's privacy, even if they are pursuing "legitimate" news. The case stems from the syndicated show *On Scene: Emergency Response*, but *COPS* exec producer John Langley says "it represents a backlash against the media."

> **JUST ASK PAT SAJAK. OR DENNIS MILLER. OR CHEVY CHASE. OR...**
Earvin "Magic" Johnson debuts his late-night talker, *The Magic Hour*, with great fanfare, only to have it canceled nine weeks later. "It's a tough game, and everyone who tries it learns that quickly," says then-NBC Entertainment prez **Warren Littlefield**.

> **REGRETTABLY, DEAN MARTIN DIDN'T LIVE TO SEE THIS DAY**
Seagram's announces its intention to acquire PolyGram for $10.6 billion.

> **HOW COOL? YOU'LL DROOL— JEWEL RULES!**
Singer **Jewel** issues a volume of poetry, called *A Night Without Armor*. It stays on best-seller lists for 11 weeks.

> **NOT SINCE CHARLTON HESTON STRAPPED ON AN AK-47 AND BEGAN DISTRIBUTING LEAFLETS OUTSIDE**
A San Francisco museum dedicated to **Barbra Streisand** closes its doors. Hello Gorgeous owner Ken

Joachim says, "There are just not enough fans."

> **BREAKING UP IS DIE-HARD TO DO**
Demi Moore and **Bruce Willis** separate—proving, says **Craig Kilborn** on *The Daily Show*, "that they've finally gotten as sick of each other as we are of them."

> **FOR ONCE IT WON'T SEEM STRANGE ON 'CHARLIE ROSE' WHEN THE HOST DOES ALL THE TALKING**
Socks the cat and **Buddy** the dog, perhaps the only current White House occupants not tainted by

Bruce and Demi kiss it all goodbye

scandal, ink a deal with Simon & Schuster to do a book of letters kids have sent them.

> YOU CAN BET BILLY RAY GAVE DAVE A BIG ACHY BREAKY HUG

Before These Crowded Streets, a new album from the **Dave Matthews Band**, hits No. 1, preventing the *Titanic* soundtrack from equaling the SoundScan-era record for the longest consecutive run at the top spot. That distinction is still held by the **Billy Ray Cyrus** debut album, *Some Gave All*.

The Clintonian pets tell their side of the story

> BUT WILL YOU RESPECT HIM IN THE EVENING?

After 11 years—and one broken nose courtesy of neo-Nazi skinheads—**Geraldo Rivera** leaves the sleaze of daytime TV to concentrate extensively on the sleaze of Washington on CNBC's *Rivera Live*.

> IMAGINE WHAT FRANK PEMBLETON WOULD HAVE GOT HIM TO ADMIT

Scott Weiland, of Stone Temple Pilots fame, is arrested in New York's Alphabet City after allegedly volunteering to a police officer that he had "just

Rivera, here with Charles Manson, leaves daytime

bought drugs." The singer is charged with trespassing and heroin possession, mere hours before he was to perform in a sold-out concert. The case was set to go to trial in December.

> YOU CAN'T ALWAYS GET WHAT YOU WANT, BUT WITH THE ADVICE OF LEADING ACCOUNTING EXPERTS, YOU CAN KEEP WHAT YOU GET

The Rolling Stones reschedule part of their Bridges to Babylon tour, reportedly to avoid paying the vast preponderance of the proceeds in taxes. This follows the news of **Keith Richards** damaging his ribs while reaching for a book in his Connecticut home. Few had predicted that Richards, a man of legendary appetites, would be felled by his reading habit.

> GIRL POWER ON THE MARCH

TIME magazine runs a cover story entitled "Is Feminism Dead?" that places **Calista Flockhart**, who plays miniskirted, self-doubting lawyer Ally McBeal, in the company of Susan B. Anthony, Betty Friedan, and Gloria Steinem, none of whom were particularly known for miniskirts or

self-doubt. Meanwhile, **Geri Halliwell** (Ginger Spice), who has been known to don the occasional miniskirt, announces she has overcome any self-doubt, and leaves the **Spice Girls** for a solo career and a gig as a U.N. Population Fund goodwill ambassador.

> BE MY, BE MY NEST EGG

Phil Spector's ex-wife, **Ronnie**, and the other Ronettes sue Spector, alleging they haven't been paid any royalties from hit records such as "Be My Baby" and "Walking in the Rain" since 1964. Spector will go on to call the case "a lot of nonsense."

> SEE, IT IS TRUE: A ROSE BY ANY OTHER NAME...

Ol' Dirty Bastard changes his name to **Big Baby Jesus**. Several weeks later, he suffers multiple gunshot wounds while being robbed.

> JUST A SIMPLE FAMILY MOMENT, SHARED BY A MILLION OR SO CLOSE FRIENDS

Nearly 1.4 million Web surfers tune in as Sean, the first baby ever to be born live over the Web, enters this world. After almost five hours, the little nipper finally comes into camera range.

THE YEAR IN REVIEW

> **Larry does not have any sense of introspection, of what the consequences of his self-absorption are on other people. I, on the other hand, have been in my introspective period since I was 14.** —GARRY SHANDLING,
> *on how he differs from his TV alter ego, Larry Sanders*

> ### READ ALL ABOUT IT: DOG BITES MAN
For the 18th time, soap diva **Susan Lucci** of *All My Children* loses out in the competition for the Daytime Emmy Awards.

> ### THE PAMELA AND TOMMY WATCH
Tommy Lee is sentenced to six months for spousal abuse and begins his prison term.

> ### AND HERE'S THE REALLY SPOOKY PART: THEY LIKE TO CALL EACH OTHER BY THEIR NAMES FROM 'GATTACA'
Parents-to-be **Ethan Hawke** and **Uma Thurman** wed May 1 at New York's Cathedral of St. John the Divine.

> ### FAMILY MATTERS
Supermodel **Cindy Crawford** weds bar owner **Rande Gerber**; **Macaulay Culkin**, 17, weds fellow actor Rachel Miner, also 17, on June 21; claiming they had sex only once or twice over 41 years, Carol

Channing seeks to end her marriage to manager Charles Lowe; **James Cameron** and his fourth wife, *Terminator* star **Linda Hamilton**, separate, and he is seen squiring *Titanic* actress **Suzy Amis**; in the "Don't Stop Believin' " department, lead singer **Steve Perry** quits Journey after two decades—the band decides to journey on with new vocalist Steve Augeri; *Friends* star **Lisa Kudrow** has a baby with adman hubby Michel Stern; **Daniel Day-Lewis** and Rebecca Miller have Arthur's grandchild; model **Paulina Porizkova** and ex-Car **Ric Ocasek** have their second child, as do the ageless **Tony Randall** and wife Heather Harlan, and **Sylvester Stallone** and Jennifer Flavin.

> ### TRIALS AND TRIBULATIONS
Quentin Tarantino is sued for $15 million by a woman who claims the actor-director struck her during a restaurant altercation with her photographer boyfriend. The case is still pending; **David Letterman** gets a speeding ticket in Montana, a state famed for having no official set speed limits in place for its wide-open highways. Unfortunately for the late-night talk-show host, he is driving in the city of Darby and is cited for doing 38 in a 25-mile-per-hour zone. Letterman pays the $50 fine; **Bob Denver** (a.k.a. Gilligan) is busted for marijuana possession. The former castaway is placed on probation after pleading no contest; former Beatle **George Harrison** announces he's recovering from throat cancer.

BUT THEN HOW DO THEY EXPLAIN THE SHOT OF ELLEN DeGENERES IN A PITH HELMET? Disney claims no sly reference to Anne Heche's sexuality was intended by the trailer to *Six Days, Seven Nights*, which shows Heche and costar Harrison Ford standing in a tropical river as Heche screams, "Some sort of creature has just swum up my pants," and a voice-over intones, "This summer, find adventure in the most remote place known to man."

july | august

> "If older men are less grumpy and embarrassed, they won't make as many wars, be so evil to people and so power mad."
> —**ROCKER LIZ PHAIR** *on why she thinks Viagra is a good thing*

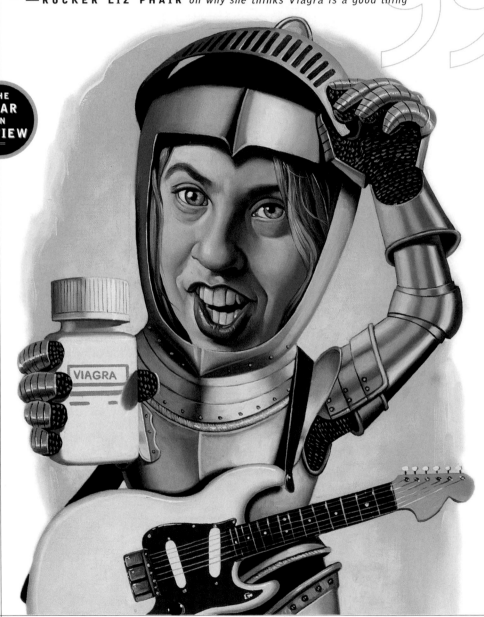

THE YEAR IN REVIEW

grave in Fairmount, Ind., is found when a sheriff's deputy drives over it on a country road. Police believe the headstone was taken as part of a teen prank. The car is seriously damaged, but the headstone sustains only a chip in one corner.

> DUMPTY, UNFOR-TUNATELY, WAS UNAVAILABLE, HAVING ALREADY BEEN COMMITTED TO SERVE AS A METAPHOR FOR NEWT GINGRICH
Director **Tony Kaye** resorts to some bizarre stunts to protest the editing of his film, *American History X.* In addition to taking out cryptically worded ads in trade magazines, Kaye shows up at a meeting with New Line Cinema president **Michael De Luca** accompanied by a priest, a rabbi, and a monk. When New Line refuses to extend Kaye's editing deadline, he unsuccessfully demands that the credits be changed to read "directed by Humpty Dumpty."

> PEOPLE WERE PROBABLY JUST TRYING TO GET A BREAK FROM THE CYNICISM OF WASHINGTON
In the week after sex-scandal-besieged **Bill Clinton** orders U.S. bomber and missile attacks on terrorist targets in Africa and Afghanistan, rentals of the video *Wag the Dog* experience a tremendous boost.

> DID ANYONE NOTICE?
Nick Evans, owner of seven CBS affiliates in the South and Midwest, temporarily pulls *Late Show With*

> DES MOINES? IOWA? JERRY, SHOULD YOU EVER FEEL A NEED TO REVIEW YOUR REP- RESENTATION...
Jerry Seinfeld decides to refund the admission price to people who attended his shows in Des Moines, Iowa, the last stop on his 1998 stand-up tour.

> HE MAY HAVE SAID 'STOP ME IF YOU'VE HEARD THIS ONE,' BUT HE PROBABLY DIDN'T MEAN IT LIKE THAT
Boston Globe columnist Mike Barnicle resigns amid charges he plagiarized **George Carlin**'s jokes and fabricated some details in his columns.

> HEADS OR TALES?
Two days after it was reported missing, the headstone from **James Dean**'s

ILLUSTRATION BY ROBERTO PARADA

David Letterman from his stations after he has trouble getting tickets to the program for friends and business associates.

> ...EXPLAINING WHY 'MONDAY NIGHT FOOTBALL' HAS BEEN SO MUCH MORE RELATION-SHIP-ORIENTED THIS SEASON

Patricia Fili-Krushel is appointed president of ABC Television Network, making her the first woman to lead a major TV network.

> TOO BAD. WE'D HAVE GIVEN A LOT TO HAVE SEEN PINOCCHIO MAKE GEPPETTO AN OFFER HE COULDN'T REFUSE

Francis Ford Coppola wins an $80 million verdict against Warner Bros. after the studio decided not to support Coppola in his efforts to make a live-action movie version of *Pinocchio*. In October, a judge will reverse the $60 million in punitive damages; later that month, Warner Bros. will appeal the $20 million in compensatory damages.

> AS PART OF THE SETTLEMENT, THE SERIES HAS TO BE RETITLED 'THE MEAN, UNPLEASANT, NASTY GOURMET'

The Frugal Gourmet (Jeff Smith) settles a sexual-harassment suit filed by seven former employees (all men) of his now defunct restaurant, who allege that he abused, assaulted, and intimidated them from the mid-1970s through 1992. Smith denies the charges, but settles (without admitting any wrongdoing) to prevent the trial from going forward; the suit is dismissed.

> PROVING THAT YOU DON'T GET TO BE A NO. 1 PROGRAM WITHOUT APPEALING TO THAT ALL-IMPORTANT NUTTY-LITERARY-RECLUSE DEMOGRAPHIC

Joyce Maynard writes a memoir, *At Home in the World*, in which she discusses her teenage romance with a much older J.D. Salinger, revealing that he taught her to induce vomiting after eating junk food and that he

loved *The Andy Griffith Show* and *I Love Lucy*.

> GEE, THE LIFE SPAN OF A FRUIT FLY IS 21 DAYS

Veteran Hollywood producer Robert Evans, 68, and actress Catherine Oxenberg, 36, announce 15 days after marrying that they are seeking to have their spur-of-the-moment marriage annulled.

> WHEN A FROSTY GLARE AND THE SILENT TREATMENT AREN'T QUITE ENOUGH

Blaze magazine editor in chief Jesse Washington says the Fugees' Wyclef Jean pulled a gun on him in retaliation for an unfavorable album review. Jean denies the allegation on MTV.

> HE ALSO WANTS YOU TO REFER TO THE HAIR BY YOUR EARS ONLY AS 'WHISKERS'

Writer-director-actor Ed Burns (*She's the One*) is forced to list his screen credit for *Saving Private Ryan* as Edward Burns because television actor Edd ("Kookie") Byrnes is claiming sole rights to the shortened version of the name. Byrnes, whose real

BROUGHT BACK THE TOUPEE, TOO There *are* second acts in American lives. After watching his career fade since pleading guilty to a misdemeanor count of sexual assault and battery in 1997, Marv Albert is rehired by the MSG Network to host TV's *SportsDesk* and call Knicks games on the radio—leaving many fans to wonder, would his commentary have the same bite?

Ethan and Uma, with baby Maya Ray and Uma's mother in Central Park

I just autographed it

and sent it back. —**RAY LIOTTA**, *on the plastic horse's head that Tina Sinatra sent him after learning he was playing her father, Frank Sinatra, in the HBO movie* The Rat Pack

The freaks come out at night: Howard teams up with CBS

name is Breitenberger, is best known for his role on the 1958–64 television series *77 Sunset Strip.*

> **HAD THEY BUT KNOWN HOW FEW PEOPLE WERE ACTUALLY GOING TO SEE THE PICTURE, THEY MIGHT NOT HAVE BOTHERED**
Fearing that they are portrayed as terrorists, Arab-American and Islamic-rights groups protest the film *The Siege.*

> **IF TRUE, IT WOULD MEAN, AMONG OTHER THINGS, THAT DOUGLAS HAS SOME NASTY SLICE IN HIS SWING**
A $155 million suit is filed in federal court alleging that in October 1997, **Michael Douglas** hit a golf ball that struck a caddie in the groin, resulting in an

injury requiring the removal of one testicle. In the complaint, caddie James Parker claims that Douglas then stuffed a small sum of money in his pocket, made a racial statement, and walked away. Douglas denies the charges, and a trial date is set for the spring.

> **HIS FIRST ASSIGNMENT: BOOK A TEE TIME WITH SADDAM HUSSEIN**
Michael Douglas is appointed a U.N. messenger of peace by the secretary-general.

> **CHARLIE ROSE, OF COURSE, IS THE FRESHLY LAUNDERED UNDERPANTS OF LATE NIGHT**
Howard Stern's new TV show debuts opposite

Saturday Night Live. The *L.A. Times* describes it as "the smelly underpants of late-night television."

> **...WHO THREATENED TO REVEAL TO THE WORLD THAT HIS WIFE WAS A MODESTLY TALENTED ACTRESS WITH A BOOB JOB**
Antonio Banderas drops out of a movie about the founder of modern Turkey, apparently bowing to pressure from Greek Americans.

> **YES, BUT NOW HE PLAYS MR. CRABAPPLE, THE CRANKY OLD MAN NEXT DOOR**
Luke Perry, whose hoped-for career as a movie hunk failed to materialize after he left *Beverly Hills, 90210*, announces his return to the show.

> **YEAH—THEY PROBABLY GOT PONIES FOR CHRISTMAS, TOO**
All Saints, the girl group that is a personal favorite of **Princes William** and

Harry, appear at a benefit concert for the Prince's Trust.

> **WE'RE JUST GUESSING, BUT IF PHOEBE, RACHEL, OR MONICA LEAVE, THEY WON'T BE REPLACED BY COURTNEY**
Courtney Love is outraged that **Billy Corgan** (lead singer of the Smashing Pumpkins) is being given so much credit for his contribution to her band's new album, *Celebrity Skin*. Corgan shrugs off her criticism, reportedly saying, "She's embarrassed that she needed someone to help her."

> **WE WERE THINKING De NIRO, PESCI, AND KEITEL AS THE KIDNAPPERS, AND ADAM SANDLER AS FRANK JR.**
After two of the three men who kidnapped him in 1963 sell the movie rights to their story for a reported $1.5 million, **Frank Sinatra Jr.** secures a preliminary injunction to prevent Columbia Pictures from

All Saints' day with Prince Charlie

HONK IF YOU LOVE CLINTON She had already bid adieu to the 'do that didn't and unveiled a newly straightened smile. But when Paula Jones, the President's most prominent accuser, was seen leaving the office of a Park Avenue plastic surgeon on July 18 wrapped in bandages, we knew something even bigger was in the offing. Jones, who reportedly sold exclusive rights to her new nose to *PrimeTime Live* and the *National Enquirer* (she's shown here prepping for her *Enquirer* shoot), said she underwent the $9,000 procedure because she was tired of people making fun of her appearance. Now, about those nails...

making any payments to his abductors.

> ### AND THAT'S WHY HE'S STILL THE KING OF THE WORLD
Leonardo DiCaprio grants the wish of gymnast Sang Lan, paralyzed in a fall at the Goodwill Games, by visiting her in her Manhattan hospital room.

> ### PAMELA AND TOMMY LEE WATCH
Tommy Lee is sentenced to 30 days for assaulting a security guard.

> ### FAMILY MATTERS
Barbra Streisand weds James Brolin on July 1; Kathy Najimy of *Veronica's Closet* weds former *Stomp* performer Dan Finnerty, Aug. 8—they have a 20-month-old child, Samia; CNN and *60 Minutes* international correspondent Christiane Amanpour and State Department spokesman James Rubin also marry on Aug. 8; it's reported that supermodel Linda Evangelista and actor Kyle MacLachlan have split; Anna Murdoch files for divorce from media-mogul husband Rupert, July 21; Ethan Hawke and Uma Thurman welcome their first daughter, Maya Ray, July 9; Jodie Foster's new son, Charles, is born at 5:53 a.m. on July 20, weighing in at 7 pounds 8 ounces. Foster, still mum on the subject of the child's father, says she'll raise him as a single mom.

> ### TRIALS AND TRIBULATIONS
Actor Woody Harrelson appears at an appellate hearing for his father, an accused professional hitman who is serving two life sentences for assassinating a federal judge—the hearing is expected to resume in March; Scott Weiland, of Stone Temple Pilots fame, disappears after failing to show up at an L.A. courthouse where he was due to face a 1996 drug charge—he later pleads guilty to one count of heroin possession and is sentenced to three years' probation in addition to enrollment in a drug-treatment program for one year; French actor Gérard Depardieu, seriously injured in a motorcycle crash outside Paris in May, is given a three-month suspended sentence, fined $1,600, and has his license revoked for 15 months because his blood-alcohol content was three times the legal limit at the time of the crash; Mikhail Markhasev is given life in prison without parole for murdering Ennis Cosby (son of Bill Cosby). The jury deliberated for less than six hours. An appeal is pending.

THE YEAR IN REVIEW

"Like all low-budget porn, the audio was terrible and it took way too long to get to the good parts." —**CRAIG KILBORN**, *commenting on President Clinton's videotaped testimony in the Lewinsky case*

THE YEAR IN REVIEW

Clinton Testimony

HINDFELD

MISS NUDE

HOT ACTION

BUSTIN THRU

Mr. Peeper

Secrets

SWING

The 1998 MTV Video Music Awards wearing Vaishnava tilak, a holy facial marking that represents purity, the World Vaishnava Association demands an apology, saying "By wearing this sacred marking while wearing clothing through which her nipples were clearly visible and while gyrating in a sexually suggestive manner with her guitar player, Madonna offended Hindus and Vaishnavas throughout the world."

> **WELL, WHEN THEY TOLD HER SHE WAS GOING TO HAVE TO WAIT TABLES TWO NIGHTS A WEEK...** Claudia Schiffer bails out of her investment in the reportedly financially troubled Fashion Cafe.

> **HEY, IF IT WAS FINANCIAL ACUMEN THAT ATTRACTED HIM, THE PRESIDENT WOULD HAVE HAD AN AFFAIR WITH ALAN GREENSPAN** Oprah Winfrey passes on a chance to interview Monica Lewinsky because the scandal-tarred former intern

Seinfeld and Sklar out shopping

> **OH, SO *THAT'S* WHAT JOEY BUTTAFUOCO HAS IN HIS HAIR** Independent producer **Vince Offer** sues *There's Something About Mary*'s writer-directors **Bobby and Peter Farrelly**, its producers, and Twentieth Century Fox, claiming that more than a dozen scenes in the 1998 comedy were lifted from his film *The Underground Comedy Movie* (which included a cameo by **Joey Buttafuoco**). A hearing is set for Jan. 11.

> **IDLE HANDS ARE THE DEVIL'S WORKSHOP** Newly unemployed comedian **Jerry Seinfeld** finds a way to keep busy. Reportedly within days of meeting Jessica Sklar—then the newlywed bride of Eric Nederlander, scion of a New York theater family— Seinfeld and Sklar are seen out and about in Manhattan. Shortly thereafter, a divorce is in the works.

> **NOT THAT THEY WERE LOOKING, MIND YOU** After **Madonna** performs on

FREE KEIKO It's been a long, hard road for *Free Willy* star Keiko the whale. First, he languished for 11 years in a cramped, tepid tank at a Mexico City theme park, covered with viral warts. Then animal lovers moved him to a rehab center in Oregon and nursed him back to health. Finally, on Sept. 10, Keiko was airlifted to Iceland, where he will swim in a floating sea pen until ready to be set free. Commenting on the more than $14 million project, Norwegian member of parliament (and former head of the Norwegian Whalers' Association) Steinar Bastesen deemed it "a lunatic waste of money. There are more than enough killer whales around; we don't need to import them. Anyway, the only good killer whale is a dead one."

asked for money. **Roseanne** offers Lewinsky several million dollars. In the end, Lewinsky agrees to talk to **Barbara Walters** for free.

> HE'LL STAND BY, JUST NOT CLOSE BY
Journalist **Kristi Witker** and two other women allege that author **C. David Heymann** fabricated the stories of affairs between them and **Robert Kennedy** for his new bio, *RFK*. Heymann insists that he stands "by every word in that book."

> IF ONLY THIS HAD HAPPENED TO 'ISHTAR'
Reels of footage from the upcoming **Warren Beatty/Diane Keaton/Goldie Hawn** comedy *Town and Country* disappear from a delivery van in New York. When they don't turn up,

New Line Cinema is forced to reshoot the scenes.

> WHY—DO THEY WANT TO START A WAR?
A survey shows that a sizable percentage of young people would rather go without food than music, and that if they had to select an ambassador to aliens from another planet, they would choose **Madonna.**

> GRUMPY OLD SPACEMEN
Ex-astronauts who haven't been invited to take a ride on the shuttle sound off about **John Glenn**'s valedictory orbital junket. **Frank Borman** says: "John Glenn, a payload specialist? That's bulls---.... NASA could get better data monitoring him for 10 days in bed." **Wally Schirra**

notes, "I can think of several more senators we should boost into space."

> THE BIG QUESTION: WHEN CARREY GOES BACK TO BEING CARREY, DOES HE STILL HAVE A PAIN IN HIS NECK?
On the set of *Man on the Moon*, the new biopic about **Andy Kaufman**, **Jim Carrey**, deep in character as Kaufman, provokes pro wrestler **Jerry Lawler**, just as Kaufman had done in 1982. And, just as he had responded in 1982, Lawler gives Carrey-as-Kaufman a neck injury that requires a brace for a week.

> PORNO FOR PYROS
The Starr Report is released over the Internet on Sept. 11, causing unprecedented

traffic jams as curious scandal buffs clog the Web.

> MAN CANNOT LIVE BY 'THE STARR REPORT' ALONE
The Columbus, Ohio, headquarters of Victoria's Secret is deluged with irate calls (mostly from men) when the intimate apparel company says it's cutting the number of catalog issues it mails out each year. A company spokeswoman promises no one will be trimmed off the list.

> THANKFULLY, UNPRECEDENTED INTERNET TRAFFIC JAMS DO NOT MATERIALIZE
Nude photos of the family-values-touting radio psychologist **Dr. Laura Schlessinger**, taken by a man with whom she had an extramarital

Philbin gets 'Stoned'

> **WE'D LIKE TO SEE AUSTIN TRY TO PULL THAT AGAINST KATHIE LEE**
Regis Philbin of *Live With Regis & Kathie Lee* is inadvertently hit in the nose while sparring on air with World Wrestling Federation champ **Stone Cold Steve Austin**. No rematch date has been set.

> **SURPRISINGLY, SOMEONE LISTENED TO HIM**
UPN attracts much attention (most of it negative) with *The Secret Diary of Desmond Pfeiffer*, a sitcom set inside the Lincoln White House, starring **Chi**

McBride as the President's African-American butler and secret adviser. Saying the show trivializes slavery, the **Rev. Jesse Jackson** joins a protest outside the gates of Paramount Studios after its premiere, with the crowd yelling, "Just say no. Just stop it."

> **PRESUMABLY THIS WOULD ALSO PREVENT THE PRESIDENT FROM BEING LISTED AS 'BUTT-HEAD' CLINTON**
Grandpa Al Lewis of *The Munsters*, running for governor in New York on the Green party line, files suit against the State Board of Elections for refusing to list him on the

ballot as *Grandpa*. He loses the suit—and come November, he is defeated.

> **NOW WE'RE WAITING FOR THE PERFORMER WHO'LL CALL HIS ALBUM 'SHUT'**
Music heavyweights **R.E.M.** and **Peter Gabriel** both plan albums with the title *Up*. Punk-folkie **Ani DiFranco** plans to

call her next album *Up Up Up Up Up Up*.

> **IN HER NEXT BOOK, A MIDDLE-AGED WOMAN WINS LOTTO, FINDS A CURE FOR CANCER, AND BECOMES THE QUEEN OF THE SOLAR SYSTEM**
Terry McMillan's 1996 novel, *How Stella Got Her Groove Back*, about a

50 YEARS OF TV IN FOUR HOURS At the Emmys on Sept. 13, Andre Braugher is recognized as Best Actor (at last!) for his final season on *Homicide: Life on the Street* (1); the *Frasier* gang accept their record fifth straight Emmy (2); Camryn Manheim proclaims, "This is for all the fat girls!" as she clutches her Best Supporting Actress trophy for *The Practice* (3); Gary Sinise wins for *George Wallace*, only to learn hours later that Wallace had died that day (4); and comic elder statesmen Milton Berle, Bob Hope, and Sid Caesar get a standing ovation (5)

woman in her 40s who meets a 20-year-old student while vacationing in Jamaica, is made into a film. Later, the 46-year-old McMillan weds Jonathan Plummer, the twentysomething student whom *she* met three years ago on vacation in Jamaica.

> IMAGINE: AN ACTRESS GETTING IN TROUBLE FOR LYING ABOUT HER AGE

Actress-screenwriter **Riley Weston** admits that she's 32 years old, rather than 19, the age she passed herself off as to her agent, many colleagues, the press, Disney Touchstone Television (which gave the putative wunderkind a six-figure development deal—now reportedly being reconsidered), and the producers of the WB teen drama *Felicity* (for which she wrote and guest-starred in an episode).

> PAMELA AND TOMMY LEE WATCH

Tommy Lee is released early from his six-month sentence for spousal abuse, on Sept. 5.

> AND LOOK FOR ANOTHER COMING ATTRACTION: MR. OVITZ'S COSTLY OUSTER

Though protesters hired a plane to fly over Disney World's Magic Kingdom in May to object to the closing of Mr. Toad's Wild Ride (which has been oper-

ating since 1971), it does them no good—the ride closes Sept. 7, and a new Winnie-the-Pooh ride is now under construction.

> MOST WENT TO MEMBERS OF JAMES CAMERON'S IMMEDIATE FAMILY

Weary of *Titanic* hoopla, one Peter Shankman manufactures a T-shirt that reads: "It sank. Get over it." In less than two days in Times Square, he sells 500 of them at $10 apiece.

It sank. Get over it.

> IT'S GOOD TO KNOW THAT IF THIS ACTING THING DOESN'T WORK OUT, TOM CAN ALWAYS FALL BACK ON A CAREER IN EMERGENCY SERVICES

Tom Cruise extends his career of heroic acts by rushing to the aid of London mugging victim Rita Simmonds. This continues a run in which he has come to the aid of a boat in distress, saved a boy from being crushed at a movie premiere, and administered first aid to a hit-and-run victim.

> YOU HAVE TO WONDER IF THESE BOYS EVER HEARD OF 'MIR'

The Russian parliament reportedly grills the State Cinematography Committee about why it allowed

the movie *Armageddon* to be released in the former Soviet Union, when "it showed the achievements of Soviet and Russian technology in the most mocking way." In one scene, a Russian space station explodes because of a leaky pipe, and in others, the only Russian cosmonaut is portrayed as bumbling and disheveled.

> FAMILY MATTERS

Sportscaster **Marv Albert** weds his long-suffering fiancée, TV producer Heather Faulkiner, on Sept. 9; model **Rebecca Romijn** and actor **John Stamos** marry on Sept. 19; actor **Brendan Fraser** marries his *George of the Jungle* costar, Afton Smith, on Sept. 27; *Today*

show hunk **Matt Lauer** weds model **Annette Roque** on Oct. 3; *Scream* costars **Courteney Cox** and **David Arquette** get engaged.

> TRIALS AND TRIBULATIONS

Arnold Schwarzenegger sues the gossip tabloid *Globe* for a story in which he is portrayed as having chronic heart trouble. The case is pending; Margaret Ray, the woman who stalked **David Letterman**, stole his Porsche, and was arrested numerous times for harassing him, commits suicide by kneeling in front of an onrushing train; *Ally McBeal*'s **Calista Flockhart** is sued by a New York law firm for alleged breach of contract. The firm claims Flockhart agreed to pay them 5 percent of her earnings in exchange for negotiating her contract with David E. Kelley Productions. The case is pending.

THE YEAR IN REVIEW

Cruise and the scene of the crime

"Writers never realize it, but the world is not out there wait-ing for your next book. The world honestly isn't paying attention. I couldn't afford to spend 11 years on this book."

—**TOM WOLFE,** *on his new novel,* A Man in Full, *for which the world has been waiting for more than two years*

intern **Monica Lewinsky** signs with British publish-er Michael O'Mara Books for a reported $600,000 advance to tell her side of the Sexgate saga. The book, tentatively titled *Monica's Story,* will be written by Princess Diana biographer **Andrew Morton** and will be published in the U.S. by St. Martin's Press.

> OF COURSE THEY WERE PUSHED OUT. FLOGGING IS ILLEGAL.

Universal Studios chair-man-CEO **Frank Biondi Jr.** is ousted after a just-okay $15 million opening week-end for the $90 million *Meet Joe Black,* which capped a year of flops that included *Blues Brothers 2000* and *BASEketball.* Two weeks later, after the equally pricey *Babe: Pig in the City* buys the farm in its bow, Universal Pictures chairman-CEO **Casey Sil-ver** resigns under pressure.

> MAYBE ELLEN WILL OPEN A LITTLE BOOKSTORE. ANNE CAN OPERATE THE ESPRESSO MACHINE.

Ellen DeGeneres tells the *Los Angeles Times* that she and partner **Anne Heche** are leaving Hollywood and quitting show business for

> SOUNDS LIKE SOMEBODY WAS WAITING FOR KEVIN'S AUTOGRAPH AND GOT A BRUSH-OFF

A new album from elec-tronic artist **DJ B-Side** called *Player 1 Press Start* includes a letter ad-dressed to **Kevin Costner** that reads, in part, "All the movies you've been in have sucked. You have sucked in them," and de-mands that he retire. A publicist for the record la-bel, Junior High Record-ings, defends the song as "a political statement" and

says Costner was chosen because he represents the bloated star system.

> WHAT'S LEFT TO FIND OUT? THE TOPPINGS ON THE PIZZA?

Ending months of specula-tion, former White House

Anne and Ellen

YEAH, BUT THAT DOESN'T MEAN THAT THEY WANT A BIG MAC OR A LUMINA FOR PRESIDENT Using the slogan "Retaliate in '98," ex–pro wrestler and Reform party candidate **Jesse "The Body" Ventura**, above, stuns political experts by winning the governor's race in Minnesota. Evidently inspired by Ventura, **Hulk Hogan** announces that he plans to run for President in the year 2000. "People know Hulk Hogan like they know McDonald's and Chevrolet," Hogan says.

"at least a year" because they're frustrated with the cold reception they've faced since coming out.

> UM...WOMEN?
In the video for his new song "Outside," **George Michael** parodies his 1998 conviction for committing a lewd act in a public rest-room. In the video, a bathroom morphs into a disco while Michael, dressed as a cop, sings

about the joys of sex in the great outdoors and dances with some scantily clad women.

> FURTHER PROOF THAT AMERICA'S TOP INTELLIGENCE OFFICIAL SHOULD BE KITTY KELLEY
Seven months after his death, the FBI releases 1,275 pages of its 1,300-page file on **Frank Sinatra**. The file contains

longtime rumors about the singer's Mob ties, explains why he never served in World War II (he was rejected as 4-F because of a perforated eardrum and "emotional instability"), and mentions an early arrest for seduction, later changed to adultery and subsequently dismissed.

> JUST THINK: IN A FEW MONTHS, THE NAMES QUI-GON JINN, MACE WINDU, AND JAR JAR WILL BE AS WELL KNOWN TO YOU AS THOSE OF MOE, LARRY, AND CURLY
The two-minute trailer for May 1999's *Star Wars: Episode I—The Phantom Menace* comes out, prompting almost as much analysis as the Zapruder film and supplying an unexpected audience of geeky comic-book-store clerks for *Meet Joe Black*.

> HE WANTED TO GET BACK TO WHERE THE GAMES ARE PLAYED *ON* DIRT, NOT *WITH* IT
Less than two years after fleeing the ESPN anchor desk for his own show at MSNBC, acerbic announcer **Keith Olbermann** exits again, this time going to Fox Sports Net for a reported $1 million, a hefty $350,000 raise over his reported MSNBC salary.

> OF COURSE, IF HE REALLY WANTED TO CUT OUT THE MIDDLEMAN, HE COULD JUST VISIT THEIR HOMES
Frasier star **Kelsey Grammer** and his wife of 16 months, Camille, set up a personal website (www.KelseyLive.com) so

they can "communicate directly with people and eliminate the 'middle man.'"

> THEY *SHOULD* HAVE BANNED IT BECAUSE IT'S A RIDICULOUS SONG TO MARCH TO
Members of the Fort Zumwalt North High School marching band in O'Fallon, Mo., sue the school authorities on free-speech grounds over the right to play an instrumental version of the 1967 **Jefferson Airplane** hit "White Rabbit" as part of a medley of '60s tunes at field shows. Authorities had banned the song because of its references to drugs. A trial date is set for May.

> WE'RE STILL WAITING TO HEAR WHETHER LBJ WAS INVOLVED
ABC and TNT drop **Oliver Stone**'s *Declassified*, a TV docudrama including an exposé of the investigation into the 1996 TWA Flight 800 crash.

> ESPECIALLY IF SHE WAS SINGING 'SUPERCALIFRAGILIS-TICEXPIALIDOCIOUS'
Director **Blake Edwards** reveals that his wife, *The Sound of Music* and *Victor/Victoria* star **Julie Andrews**, will likely never sing again because of throat surgery in 1997 to

Winslet and Threapleton

THE YEAR IN REVIEW

remove noncancerous nodules. At the time, doctors said her voice would return within six weeks. But, says Edwards, "if you heard [her voice], you'd weep."

> AND YET 'A NIGHT AT THE ROXBURY' WAS ALLOWED TO REACH AUDIENCES UNIMPEDED BY ANY GOVERNMENT AGENCY

A working print of the Universal thriller *Virus*, being sent in a box labeled "Virus—OK Bud Smith #1" aboard a jet from Toronto's Deluxe Laboratories to the L.A. office of director John Bruno, vanishes when the plane lands. "When the U.S. Customs officers saw *Virus* on the box," says Smith, "they [suspected hazardous material] and called in the FDA." He later found the print in quarantine in Memphis.

> THE STUDENTS, ALL OF WHOM ATTENDED BEVERLY HILLS HIGH...

A study funded in part by the Directors Guild of America concludes that teenagers who spend most of their free time on movies, television, and music are getting lessons in creativity when they immerse themselves in popular culture.

> MILLIONS OF MEN WHO DON'T KNOW THE DIFFERENCE BETWEEN A SALCHOW AND A LUTZ CAN NOW PICK HER BREASTS OUT OF A LINEUP

Former Olympic ice-skating gold medalist **Katarina Witt** bares all for *Playboy*.

> DISCUSSING, NO DOUBT, A SQUEEZE PLAY

Sports announcers **Joe Buck, Bob Brenly,** and **Tim McCarver** are heard

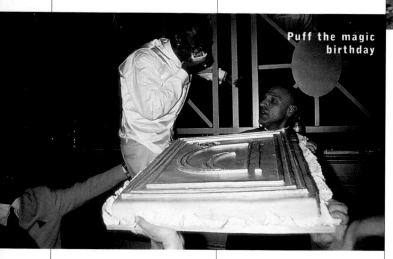

Puff the magic birthday

> AND IF THIS WORKS, 'CATS'!

Roger Daltrey, 54, lead singer for the Who, takes on the role of Scrooge in the Theater at Madison Square Garden's production of *A Christmas Carol: The Musical*.

calling a baseball game in the background of the **Linda Tripp** tapes.

> GIVE IT TO SOMEONE YOU LOVE. TELL HER SHE'S WORTH IT.

Just in time for the holi-

days, **Miss Piggy** launches her own porcine fragrance, appropriately called Moi. Say spokespeople for this egotistical Muppet, "Elegance and sex appeal transcend species."

> TRUE, 'BELOVED' ISN'T QUITE THE ARTISTIC ACHIEVEMENT THAT THE NEW 'HOLLYWOOD SQUARES' IS...

At a Harvard lecture, **Whoopi Goldberg** reportedly snickers in response to a question about whether **Oprah Winfrey**'s portrayal in the media as the ideal black woman was accurate, then explains, "Something flew up my nose." When asked what she thought of

Beloved, Goldberg responds, "I know if I answer you truthfully, I'll have to answer for it in the media, and I don't want to get into that with her."

> MAKES YOU WONDER WHAT WAS REALLY IN THOSE ISAAC SPECIALS

The **Pacific Princess** cruise ship, the floating set of TV's original *Love Boat*, is held at a Greek port after two crew members are arrested, allegedly with 56 pounds of heroin in their cabin.

> HEY, A FREE MEAL IS A FREE MEAL

Responding to **Sean "Puffy" Combs'** celeb-

> **I've really given up my** life to God, and I know that's why I'm OK and at peace.... It's not that I never talk about it (religion). It's just that it doesn't go with what people want to think of me as. **—SHARON STONE**

packed video invitation, more than 1,000 luminaries, including **Mariah Carey**, **Chris Rock**, and **Sarah, Duchess of York**, mob the rapper-producer's 28th-birthday bash in New York City.

> MONGKUT: LIKE EISNER, EXCEPT WITHOUT THE CLOUT

Thailand's Film Board refuses to let Twentieth Century Fox shoot a remake of

Gettin' jiggy with Miss Piggy and Moi

the 1946 film *Anna and the King of Siam* on location in that country, saying that the script insults the revered 19th-century king Mongkut, an offense punishable there by 3 to 15 years in prison.

> THANKFULLY, THE 'YOU'VE GOT MAIL' ACTION FIGURE COMES WITH OPTIONAL HELMET AND SUBMACHINE-GUN ACCESSORIES

DreamWorks puts the kibosh on Hasbro's plan for

an action figure based on **Tom Hanks**' character from *Saving Private Ryan*, deeming it inappropriate.

> FUNNY—ONE DOESN'T USUALLY ASSOCIATE ADAM SANDLER WITH IRONY

"Don't use crack," former New York Giants linebacker **Lawrence Taylor** (who plays a football coach in **Adam Sandler**'s hit *The Waterboy*) exhorts team members in the movie. Shortly before the film's November release, however, Taylor is arrested in Florida on crack cocaine charges. He pleads not guilty but reportedly later enters a rehab facility.

> TRIALS AND TRIBULATIONS

Producer-director **James Orr**, 44, is sentenced to three years' probation for beating and choking ex-girlfriend **Farrah Fawcett**, 51, in January 1998. Orr had been convicted in August on one count of battery; supermodel **Kate Moss** reportedly checks herself into London's Priory Clinic for exhaustion, Nov. 4. According to newspaper reports, Moss is trying to recover from fatigue brought on by her jet-set lifestyle; actor **Tommy Lee Jones** injures himself falling from a horse during a polo game; the Orange County appeals court re-

verses a 1996 lower-court decision granting **O.J. Simpson** custody of Sydney, 13, and Justin, 10, his two children by Nicole Brown Simpson. The court reportedly orders a new hearing to determine whether Simpson has a "propensity towards violence." Nicole's parents' lawyer had argued that the lower court had failed to consider both their daughter's murder and evidence of spousal abuse during the marriage; **Michael J. Fox**, 37, reveals in a cover story in PEOPLE magazine that he is suffering from Parkinson's disease. Fox says he first noticed symptoms in 1991, while filming the movie *Doc Hollywood*; Super Freaky ex-con **Rick James**, 50, suffers a major stroke, probably brought on by a blood vessel in his neck bursting during a Denver concert Nov. 9.

> FAMILY MATTERS

In his fifth trip down the aisle, **Tony Curtis** weds Jill Vanden Berg, Nov. 6, in Las Vegas, with daughter **Jamie Lee** looking on; *Titanic*'s Rose, **Kate Winslet**, 23, marries assistant film director Jim Threapleton, 24, Nov. 22 in Reading, England; *CNN NewsStand* coanchor **Willow Bay** and her hubby, ABC president **Bob Iger**, welcome their first child, Robert, on Nov. 3; country-music queen **Wynonna Judd** files for divorce from yacht salesman Arch Kelley III after two kids and almost three years of marriage; **Linda Hamilton** files for divorce from *Titanic* director **James Cameron**, Dec. 14.

JACK IN THE BOX *60 Minutes* broadcasts a mercy killing by "Dr. Death" **Jack Kevorkian** (below, with correspondent Mike Wallace), prompting an outcry by media critics. Kevorkian says his goal was to be arrested so he could bring the issue of euthanasia to the courts; three days after the broadcast, he is charged with first-degree murder in Michigan. A trial date is set for March.

THE LAST LAUGH

THOSE WHO SPENT 1998 on Mars may be unaware of this, but last spring, under Pentagon-class secrecy, the final episode of *Seinfeld* was filmed. But now, at long last, the truth is out: It was not Newman who murdered Jerry, but George's mother. Just kidding. Not unexpectedly, the occasion was bittersweet for four of the most thoroughly self-absorbed sitcom characters ever and the millions of viewers who were nonetheless thoroughly absorbed by them. And while there were laughs aplenty—that's Jerry and Julia Louis-Dreyfus sharing one—other emotions were at work as well. "There was a show behind the show," said Seinfeld, confessing that even he felt, well, moved. "You're doing a scene, but there was an equally dramatic scene going on in your head. It's like those stereo-vision goggles." Later, nostalgia, in the form of scrambling acquisitiveness, took over: Louis-Dreyfus got one of the *Seinfeld* set's phones, Wayne Knight kept Newman's glasses, and Seinfeld grabbed the intercom, the booth from Monk's coffee shop, and that always-unlocked apartment door. Hey, just because a guy's rich doesn't mean he isn't sentimental. —JAMIE MALANOWSKI

SLEEPING BEAUTIES

"I'M LYING IN BED/JUST LIKE BRIAN WILSON DID," sang Canada's Barenaked Ladies on "Brian Wilson," the band's 1992 ode to the Beach Boys' resident troubled genius. But Stephen Page, Ed Robertson, Jim Creeggan, and Tyler Stewart (shown here clockwise from top left, making like their hero) don't have much time for lazing around these days; they're too busy capitalizing on the breakthrough success of *Stunt,* their fifth album (and the first to become a top 10 hit in America). The undeniable appeal of the Ladies' immensely hummable tunes—such as the inescapable smash "One Week"—hit home in a big way in '98, and the hard-touring group's live performances proved they're as entertaining to watch as they are to listen to (singer-guitarist Page somehow manages to look cool while leaping around like a portly Pete Townshend). "The way we are on stage is still incredibly honest," says Page. "It's who we are." As for the derision of all those hipper-than-thou critics who loathe the group—*fugeddaboudit*. We think Barenaked Ladies are more fun than a night at a strip club. —TOM SINCLAIR/PHOTOGRAPHS BY SIAN KENNEDY

STANTON ON PRINCIPLE

WAS THERE ANYTHING NEW to add in 1998 to the already overhyped mystique of the Bill Clinton psyche? Director Mike Nichols and his longtime collaborator, screenwriter Elaine May, thought so. They turned the best-selling roman à clef *Primary Colors* into a deft political satire starring a drawlingly dead-on John Travolta (below, on the campaign trail with Nichols) as presidential candidate Jack Stanton, a hand-shaking dichotomy whose cadre of handlers (Billy Bob Thornton, Adrian Lester, Kathy Bates) must gauge how best to rein him in before letting him loose on the public. Of course, Nichols, director of *The Graduate, Heartburn,* and *The Birdcage,* is no stranger to comedies of manners. But with this one, the former stand-up stood up for the Commander-in-Chief. "This movie is not about Clinton," he said. "It's about us—the public—and how we elect these guys." —JOE NEUMAIER

"IT'S THE KIND OF FILM I MAKE," Robert Redford has said of *The Horse Whisperer,* the first movie he directed and starred in. The Sundance auteur saw in Nicholas Evans' best-selling novel the kind of thoughtful, quiet man that fascinates him. "Tom Booker is a hero because he heals and he saves the soul of something," Redford said of his character. The people who need healing, in this case, are a hard-edged magazine editor and her grievously wounded teenage daughter (Kristin Scott Thomas and Scarlett Johansson, below), whose physical—and emotional—scars are at the heart of the story. Redford, who was so taken with the book that he locked up film rights even before it was published, said, "It touched my heart. The horse is just a metaphor. It's really about love, loss, and sacrifice." —JN

WATER BOY

R.E.M. ARE GRAYING GRACEFULLY. "I think I'm a much better writer now than when I was 22," said Michael Stipe (left), who once noted that if his first album had sold 5 million copies (like that of his friend Kurt Cobain), he'd be dead too. Instead, success came gradually to the band (over the course of 10 years), and they've cultivated a mature sound that has kept their fans coming back even as the alternative era faded. For their first release since the departure of drummer Bill Berry, R.E.M. chose the evocative title *Up.* The album uses a mixture of offbeat instruments and studio tricks to add a raw, scratchy percussion. "All the things we had been used to doing," Stipe has said of the album, "the ways we used to work in the studio, were totally thrown out the window." The result? So far, the reaction of fans seems to be, keep it *Up.* —JN/PHOTOGRAPH BY CHRISTY BUSH

JUGGLING ACT

HOW TO EXPLAIN THE RUNAWAY success of the Dave Matthews Band? In an age when artifice routinely beats art to the top of the pop charts, this offbeat quintet has sold millions of albums with its crazy-quilt blend of roots rock, fusion, world beat, bluegrass, and whatever other neglected musical genre it chooses to throw in. Led by South African expatriate Dave Matthews (center left, with band mate Stefan Lessard, center right, and crew), who sings and plays guitar, the interracial group includes Boyd Tinsley (violin), LeRoi Moore (saxophone), Carter Beauford (drums), and Lessard (bass). The band's virtuoso musicianship and weirdly compelling songs have made them a tremendous concert draw (with more than one million tickets sold during their 53-date tour last summer), and their fans are as shamelessly devoted to them as Deadheads were to Jerry & Co. in days of yore. So is the DMB phenomenon an acid-flashback fluke, or the result of some cosmic hunger for challenging, organic music? "We're much more than the sum of our parts," Matthews has said by way of explanation. "How's that for a cliché?" —TS

LAUGHING AT DEATH

TAKE AN ANGEL OF DEATH who wants to live (he's seduced by the taste of peanut butter and the charms of Claire Forlani), add a do-gooder tycoon to show him how, and you have the essence of *Meet Joe Black,* director Martin Brest's whimsical update of 1934's *Death Takes a Holiday.* But did the weighty subject matter inspire stars Brad Pitt and Anthony Hopkins (cracking up at left) to look within themselves for insights about life and death? Not really. Said Pitt: "I just kinda winged it, if you want to know the truth." —JN

HER HEART'S DESIRE

SHE MAY NOT BE SUPERWOMAN, but Oprah Winfrey is arguably the most powerful woman in America today. She even gets people to read fiction, and who else can make that claim? In 1998, moviegoers saw her incredible influence at work as Toni Morrison's *Beloved*, a challenging tale about freed blacks living in Ohio after the Civil War, came to the screen. Besides producing the film, Winfrey starred as Sethe, whose slavery-induced suffering will not give her rest. Along with director Jonathan Demme (left) and costar Danny Glover (center), she made a bold, complex movie, but one that, unfortunately, did not pull in huge audiences. Still, the film had ardent fans, including one not-so-easy-to-please novelist. "They did something I thought they never could," said Morrison. They made "the film represent not the abstraction of slavery but the individuals and consequences of it." —JM

RING-A-DING-DINGSVILLE

EVEN IF FRANK SINATRA HADN'T DIED IN MAY, the low-intensity vogue for lounge culture that began a couple years ago with *Swingers* was fated to crest this year, most particularly because of HBO's production of *The Rat Pack*, Rob Cohen's fact-chunked depiction of this boy-oh-boys' club at its smokin', drinkin', swingin', swaggerin' height. Casting was key: Ray Liotta (center) looks little, and sounds less, like Sinatra, but his interpretation of the man as a gifted, commanding, tempestuous Chairman of the Board desperate for Jack Kennedy's imprimatur was compelling. The performance by Don Cheadle (right) brought out the conflicts that Sammy Davis Jr. faced in a world, a profession, and a pack that was otherwise all white. Joe Mantegna had less to do than the others, but what he had was choice. He played Dean Martin as a man who took on aloofness to preserve his integrity. He also got the movie's best line: "One of these days everybody's gonna wake up with a heck of a hangover, down two aspirin with a glass of tomato juice, and wonder what the hell all the fuss was about." Sorry, Dino: They're still in a fuss-making phase. —JM

DRAWING THE LYNE

AUGUST WAS THE MONTH for anticlimax. Hurricane Bonnie loitered off the Carolinas, threatening all types of ferocity, then wandered away without producing any sort of theatrical cataclysm. And *Lolita* aired on Showtime. The Adrian Lyne movie, based on Vladimir Nabokov's masterful, controversial novel about a grown man's passion for a barely pubescent girl, had been knocking around Hollywood for months, waiting for a distributor willing to brave the potential onslaught of placard wavers. Eventually Showtime stepped up and announced that it would show the film, a decision that ought to have set the glassware trembling, for now it was not confined to art houses in distant downtowns, but...in our living rooms. Then *Lolita* aired, and what happened? People saw Lyne (standing) display his customary intelligence without his customary éclat, and saw quite marvelous performances from Jeremy Irons and the sensational Dominique Swain, and then went about their business. Which, you'll recall, meant talking about the President and his relationship with a much, much, much, much younger (though postpubescent) woman. Timing is everything. —J M

ONE SHOT

IT WAS QUITE A CHALLENGING year for the team responsible for *The X-Files*. First there was the little matter of the action-packed film that came out in the summer. Many movies have been inspired by TV series, and many series have inspired movies, but never has a show paused in the middle of its run to put out a feature, and one that constituted connective tissue to the episodes of the show. Then *X-Files* creator Chris Carter came up with the idea of producing an episode in real time—that is, one in which the action, captured in long, seamless takes, begins and ends within the 50-some minutes allotted for the show. (He drew inspiration from Alfred Hitchcock, whose *Rope* was essentially a stage play that involved only one set and a handful of characters.) "Triangle," as the *X-Files* episode was called, used 150 extras and climaxed in a smashing brawl. This meant a special emphasis on realism, especially in the fighting, prompting star David Duchovny (right) to complain jokingly: "The guys are manhandling me. I could win an Emmy for most bruises. I think that's one of the categories they award the week before they give out the big ones." No wonder he looks so pooped. —J M

CAN THIS BE HAPPINESS?

THEY MAY NOT BE EVERYONE'S idea of suburbanites, but the Jersey citizens depicted in Todd Solondz's *Happiness* certainly hit a nerve. Interweaving several bleak tales—most notably one about a tormented family man (Dylan Baker) who acts out his pedophilic urges on his son's schoolmates—*Happiness* turned off many moviegoers. Yet it was an indie hit. "People tell me these are ugly characters," said Solondz (above, center right, directing Lara Flynn Boyle, left). "I see them as hurt, as lost souls." With a taste for smirking little touches (including using songs like "You Light Up My Life" and Air Supply's "Lost in Love") and a blithe lack of shame, Solondz points to the pain that lies behind our split-level lives. "It is interspersed with a certain layer of hope," said Solondz, "but it's hard for many people perhaps to grasp that because they're so shocked." —JN/PHOTO-GRAPH BY HENNY GARFUNKEL

NO MORE 'FLIPPING'

THERE WAS ALWAYS A meta-quality to *The Larry Sanders Show*, a sense that the ruthless satire of showbiz egotism we were seeing came with endless subtexts, leaving us never quite sure whether the scene we were watching was brilliantly imagined or clinically transcribed. What other way, then, to end the series' six-year run than to have the last episode be—get this—the last episode? "It's a very dramatic episode," said Shandling, "in that Larry doesn't want to deal with any of the emotions.... It's not till the very end that he realizes that this show, which was his whole life, is really over, and then there's a 10- or 15-minute roller-coaster ride of emotion." The episode's A-list guests included David Duchovny, Jerry Seinfeld, Ellen DeGeneres, Warren Beatty, and Jim Carrey, but the series will always stand out for the splendidly needy ensemble it showcased weekly. Said Shandling of his work on the show: "I wanted to do a project that dealt in a deeper way with human behavior." It's a trick no prosecutor has ever mastered: how to both indict a species and leave it laughing. —JM/

PHOTOGRAPH BY JEFFERY NEWBURY

style

1998

THE YEAR'S BEST LOOKS

by DEGEN PENER

> **RETRO PLUSH** Like the rest of the globe, the style world in 1998 was enraptured with all things *Titanic*. J. Peterman sold clothes and props from the movie in its catalog; actress Gloria Stuart had a special bejeweled bag designed by Kathrine Baumann in the shape of the big ship; and circa-1912 chokers chugged back into vogue. But nothing was more beautiful than the sumptuous gowns that graced the year's biggest parties: (1) Arriving at the Oscars, Kate Winslet proved that beauty doesn't have to be bone thin. Her dress, by Alexander McQueen for Givenchy, would have looked right at home in the ocean liner's grand ballroom. (2) Always a fan of vintage looks, Winona Ryder—attending the premiere of the glam-rock flick *Velvet Goldmine* at the Cannes film festival—forwent the kitschy '70s look in favor of her usual refined style in Badgley Mischka. (3) And John Galliano for Christian Dior draped and beaded Sandra Bullock at the Golden Globes, so that even the girl next door was lavishly embellished.

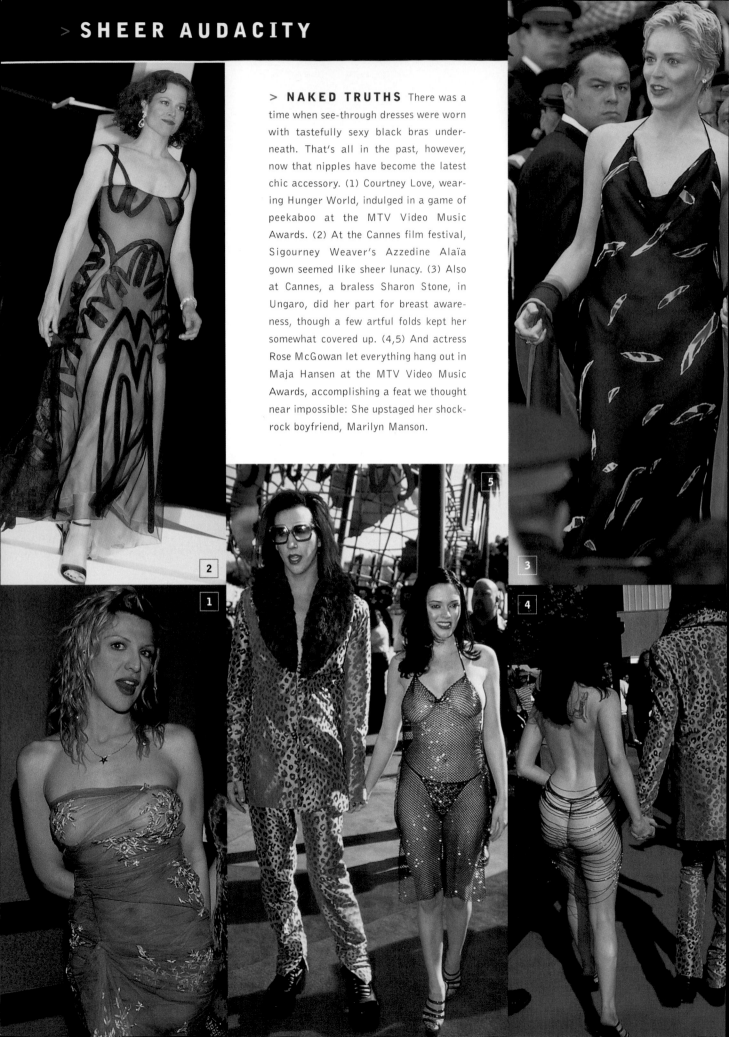

> **NAKED TRUTHS** There was a time when see-through dresses were worn with tastefully sexy black bras underneath. That's all in the past, however, now that nipples have become the latest chic accessory. (1) Courtney Love, wearing Hunger World, indulged in a game of peekaboo at the MTV Video Music Awards. (2) At the Cannes film festival, Sigourney Weaver's Azzedine Alaïa gown seemed like sheer lunacy. (3) Also at Cannes, a braless Sharon Stone, in Ungaro, did her part for breast awareness, though a few artful folds kept her somewhat covered up. (4,5) And actress Rose McGowan let everything hang out in Maja Hansen at the MTV Video Music Awards, accomplishing a feat we thought near impossible: She upstaged her shock-rock boyfriend, Marilyn Manson.

> **HOW LOW CAN THEY GO?** The backless look nearly became the butt look on a few stars as dresses sank almost to the cheek level. (1) At the MTV Movie Awards, Carmen Electra created a stir in this Stephen Sprouse number. No one could figure out how it was staying up until a band of clear plastic was spotted encircling her back. (2) Jennifer Love Hewitt, in Donna Karan, also went into reverse at the MTV Movie Awards. (3) *Titanic* actress Suzy Amis created a spinal flap at the film's Hollywood premiere. (4) And Jennifer Lopez, in Versace, showed off her much-admired backside at the VH1 Fashion Awards. The low-slung look seemed practically created for her.

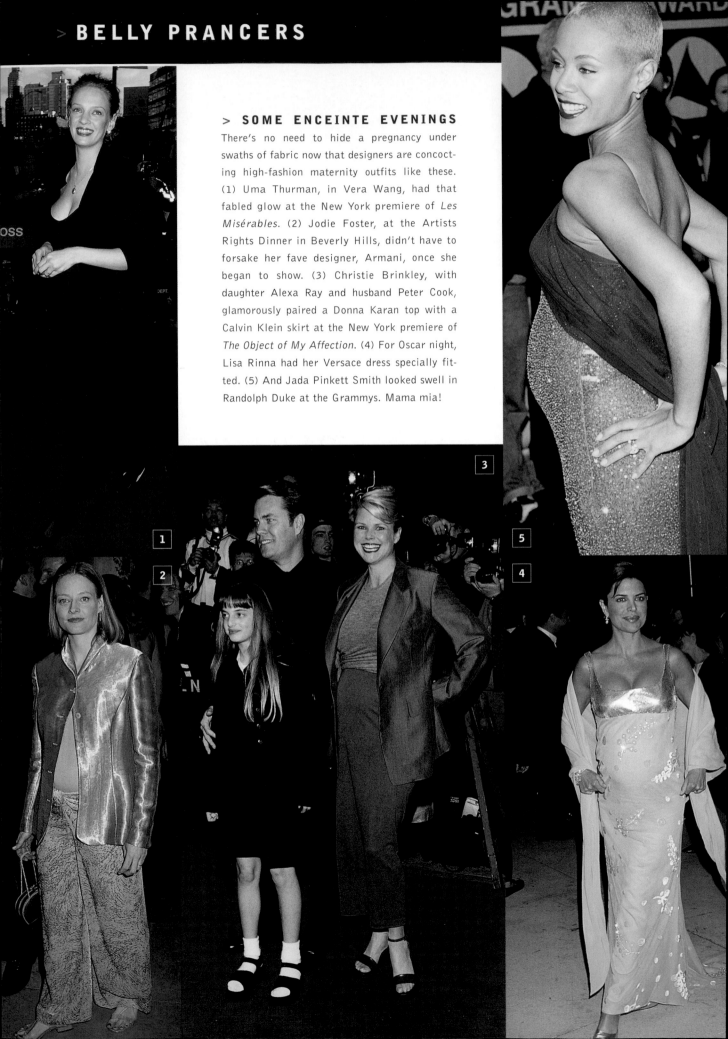

> SOME ENCEINTE EVENINGS

There's no need to hide a pregnancy under swaths of fabric now that designers are concocting high-fashion maternity outfits like these. (1) Uma Thurman, in Vera Wang, had that fabled glow at the New York premiere of *Les Misérables*. (2) Jodie Foster, at the Artists Rights Dinner in Beverly Hills, didn't have to forsake her fave designer, Armani, once she began to show. (3) Christie Brinkley, with daughter Alexa Ray and husband Peter Cook, glamorously paired a Donna Karan top with a Calvin Klein skirt at the New York premiere of *The Object of My Affection*. (4) For Oscar night, Lisa Rinna had her Versace dress specially fitted. (5) And Jada Pinkett Smith looked swell in Randolph Duke at the Grammys. Mama mia!

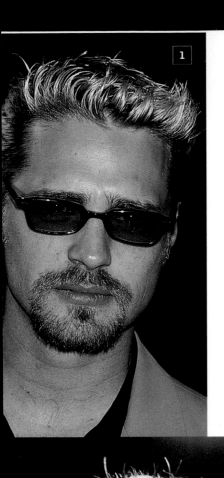

1

> **BLOND AMBITION** For some hair-brained reason, actors dipped into the peroxide bottle in 1998 as furiously as Madonna once had. But the results, with one notable exception, were a washout. (1) Jason Priestley got back to his roots at Fox's fall TV announcements. (2) At the same event, *Melrose Place*'s Rob Estes went so light he was almost unrecognizable. (3) George Clooney got glazed for the premiere of *Out of Sight*. (4) And who'da thunk it? Drew Carey, at the premiere of *Godzilla*, looked darn near natural as a bleached blond. When a trend looks good only on Carey, you've gotta wonder what's going on.

2

4 **3**

1

> **WINGING IT** No, these celebrities didn't forget to put on bug spray. It's just that butterflies became the accessory of choice in 1998. (1) Salma Hayek adopted lepidopteran decals at the MTV Video Music Awards. (2) At the premiere of *Godzilla*, Jennifer Tilly took wing in Dolce & Gabbana's dress and matching heels. (3) And Drew Barrymore—who loves butterflies so much she insisted on wearing a butterfly-appliqué denim jacket in *The Wedding Singer*—pinned another one on at Nickelodeon's Kids' Choice Awards. Is this what they mean by social butterflies?

3

2

WHOSE SARI NOW? "Thank U, India," sings Alanis Morissette on her latest album. And the fashion biz seconded that. (1) Variations of the same little Anna Sui dress—a sari-print shift in popping pink or blue—hypnotized a whole bevy of celebrities (left to right): Tyra Banks, Cindy Crawford, Sherilyn Fenn, Christina Ricci, Natasha Richardson, and *Lolita*'s Dominique Swain looked like sextuplets. (2) At the MTV Video Music Awards, Gwen Stefani of No Doubt turned Hindu-style ornamentation into mosh wear by combining it with a blue, Muppet-style bra and matching hair. (3) Naomi Campbell went subcontinental at Cannes. (4) And Madonna wore her soul on her sleeve at the MTV awards, henna-ing her hands with traditional Hindu *mehndi* tattoos. Now that's a fashion guru.

1

2

3

4

> **GRAY EXPECTATIONS** Once upon a time, the greatest fear in the fashion world was becoming the man in the proverbial gray suit. Now celebs can't get their hands on enough Gucci, Prada, and Marc Jacobs in the somber shade. (1) Brad Pitt, at the West Coast premiere of *Meet Joe Black*, eschewed his character's namesake color in favor of gray, the new black. (2) Flannel flattered Liv Tyler, in Dolce & Gabbana, at Cannes. (3) Jennifer Aniston, in Gucci, discovered the look's biggest advantage at VH1's "Divas Live" concert: no worries about how to match a skirt with a top. (4) And, true to form, Mariah Carey, wearing Chloé at the Blockbuster Awards, figured out how to take the once-staid flannel as far from its roots as possible. By the looks of that hemline, gray has come a long way from the '50s.

1 **2** **3** **4** **5** **6**

> **THAT'S A WRAP** In another sign of conservative times in fashion, three of Hollywood's most bodaciously exhibitionistic stars decided 1998 was the year to button up. (1) A pre-makeover Carmen Electra in 1996 tended to use her chest as a flashbulb magnet. (2) Cut to November 1998: At the East Coast premiere of *Meet Joe Black*, Electra restrained her charms in basic black. (3) Back when she was part of the Spice Girls in 1997, Ginger preferred such over-the-top clothes as fur chubbies, platform boots, and her signature Union Jack dress. (4) Now that she's a goodwill ambassador for the U.N. Population Fund, Ginger—uh, make that Geri Halliwell—is going for a more savory look. Here she was at the MTV Video Music Awards looking more like a corporate vice president than a pop star. (5) Pamela Anderson Lee got busted at Cannes in 1995. (6) But at the New York fashion shows last spring, a restyled Anderson Lee hid her assets. When even these women are toning it down, you know that blatant T&A is the biggest style no-no in town.

> **1998'S STYLE LOSER** Channeling the ghost of Morticia Addams wasn't the best of moves for Madonna, above. (1) She kicked off her *Ray of Light* look at the Metropolitan Museum of Art's Costume Institute Gala in December '97 with this cosmic Versace gown. (2) At January's Golden Globes, Madonna was tastefully gothic in a black Balenciaga with Pre-Raphaelite curls. (3) But by the time of the Oscars, she had gone whole-hog Anne Rice, piling on Fred Leighton jewels, an Olivier Theyskens dress, and a Jean-Paul Gaultier skirt. (4) She put a crimp in her style at the Kids' Choice Awards last April, then (5) made like a rich hippie in New York during the summer. (6) At MTV's Video Music Awards, she offended a whole new sensibility with Hindu facial markings, before (7) donning another Olivier Theyskens freak frock last October at the VH1 Fashion Awards. (8) And at the MTV Europe Music Awards, Madonna added another vintage look to her repertoire: Gloria Swanson.

> **1998'S STYLE WINNER** Here's a hint, Madonna: Make like Cameron Diaz. The *Something About Mary* girl wound up the most glamorous star of 1998 (she even won a VH1 award for Best Personal Style) by keeping her look simple and elegant. (1) At the *Wild Things* premiere, Diaz paired a luxurious gray sweater with a chic slit skirt. (2) On Oscar night, she looked gossamer in Chloé, and then (3) went sporty for April's Toyota Pro/Celebrity Race. (4) With then boyfriend Matt Dillon at the MTV Movie Awards, she found a higher clothes consciousness in a crocheted dress. (5) Her scarf jauntily topped off a Marc Jacobs top and Chloé pants at the *Mary* premiere—but (6) she showcased her fresh looks at the MTV Video Music Awards by going relatively unadorned. (7) Diaz's rope necklace, paired with a Collette Dinnigan dress, was a nice surprise at *GQ*'s Men of the Year Awards. (8) And at the premiere of *Very Bad Things*, Diaz was anything but bad in a vintage cloche hat and a Clements Ribeiro coat.

the best & worst

OPINION IS THE LOWEST FORM of knowledge, Plato taught. But what was that? His opinion! Herewith, *our* opinions on the highest achievements and lowest forms of wreckage in the pop-culture parade that was 1998. • The year in film included the profound (*Saving Private Ryan*), the disturbing (*The Truman Show*), and the profoundly disturbing (*Happiness*). (The profoundly missable? *Snake Eyes* and *Blade*.) On TV, *Buffy* slayed us, we flipped for *Larry Sanders*, and we rocked with Chris. (But it's down the tube for *Dateline NBC* and *Nash Bridges*.) The best in music looked to the past (a decades-old live performance by Bob Dylan), reevaluated the present (R.E.M., keeping it *Up*), and faced the future (in the form of a gloriously miseducated Lauryn Hill); the worst was the same old same old from Van Halen and Courtney Love. For those eager to crack open a good book, we steer you to *A Man in Full* and *Bridget Jones's Diary*. On video, a Japanese animated treasure (*Kiki's Delivery Service*) tops our list (which also includes *A Personal Journey With Martin Scorsese Through American Movies*). And rounding out this section, a multimedia heads up on hardware (the iMac), software (*Star Wars: Behind the Magic*), games (Metal Gear Solid), and gadgets (the Game Boy camera).

> by <

**OWEN
GLEIBERMAN**

SAVING PRIVATE RYAN

When I went to see Steven Spielberg's cataclysmic World War II masterpiece on opening weekend (it was my second viewing), most of the audience sat right through to the end of the closing credits. Few of us moved, or even spoke. We were too thunderstruck. Any movie that can create in its viewers this hushed and staggering a contemplation of the defining military conflict of the 20th century is nothing less than a seismic work of art. Yet such is the nature of our myopic media culture that I now feel compelled to defend Spielberg against the charge that he has filmed two extraordinary battle sequences and sandwiched some Hollywood combat clichés in between. I could go on about the performances (Tom Hanks' authority and clandestine turmoil, Jeremy Davies' terror), but the ultimate brilliance of *Saving Private Ryan* is the way it depicts the horror of World War II right alongside its heroism— indeed, the two are organically intertwined. As a vision of hell, the opening D-Day massacre may, in movie terms, rank with Picasso's *Guernica*, but when it's over, the spectre of war doesn't disappear. It haunts the soldiers' every breath. The final battle is wrenching in a less existential, more clear-eyed way. That's because the men now know each other, and they understand why they're fighting: not to save Private Ryan but to save what he stands for—the belief that another man's life is really your own.

2 HAPPINESS It's perfectly accurate to describe Todd Solondz's gleefully twisted mosaic of lust and despair as a black comedy. Somehow, though, that fails to do justice to its fearless, mordant intimacy—the cathartic feeling this filmmaker gives you that he is putting his squirmiest sick-puppy secrets right up there on screen, and that a few of those secrets may just mirror yours. The oft-quoted exchange between Lara Flynn Boyle's poet-masochist Helen and Jane Adams' waiflike Joy (Helen: "I'm not laughing at you, I'm laughing with you!" Joy: "But I'm not laughing!") incarnates Solondz's prickly fusion of cruelty and compassion. His characters may not be laughing, but we in the audience are laughing at them *and* with them: at their cluelessness, with their loneliness, at the extremes to which they'll go to dream their way out of both. Linked together, these desperate souls form a daisy chain of neurosis. To be drawn into the film is to become part of the chain—and, in Solondz's most daring gambit, to view the for-

bidden compulsions of a pedophile (played with queasy sympathy by Dylan Baker) not simply as a crime, but as a projection of the all-too-human gap between desire and fulfillment.

---

3 THE TRUMAN SHOW A nightmare that looks like a daydream, Peter Weir's hypnotic entertainment-age fairy tale enfolds you inside a television series that never stops, but the film isn't really about television. It's about the homogenized consciousness that TV makes possible, a consciousness that is currently revamping the world into an insidious consumer mirage. As Truman Burbank, a man who has spent every moment of his existence surrounded by actors, and is therefore programmed—without knowing it—to behave like one himself (literally as the star of his own life), Jim Carrey, with his pristine boyishness and question-mark soul, creates a new kind of hero, a Capra-meets-Serling zombie saint who awakens to the reality that his very imagination has been molded in

Saving Private Ryan

The Truman Show

plastic. Dismissed by some as superficial, *The Truman Show* will, I think, appear only more prophetic as time goes on.

4 **SHAKESPEARE IN LOVE** Not just a romance but a true love comedy, this effusively witty and full-bodied fancy follows the weeks during which William Shakespeare, under the spell of a sublime but doomed affair, pours his life into the art of *Romeo and Juliet*, thus giving his art the eternal blush of life. Joseph Fiennes, as the charmingly motormouthed Bard, and Gwyneth Paltrow, as his exquisite lady love, don't just have chemistry, they have *communion*, and the film celebrates Shakespeare's genius—seen, in spirit, as the forebear to the movies—with an impassioned savvy so irresistible it just about vibrates with joy.

5 **A SIMPLE PLAN** This wintry tale of ordinary men entrapped by extraordinary greed is as zigzaggy and pungent as *The Treasure of the Sierra Madre* or anything by the young Roman Polanski. Here, though, the director is Sam Raimi, erstwhile maestro of gonzo horror, now reborn as a filmmaker of thrilling psychological dexterity and craft. Three Midwestern yokels uncover a crashed plane that contains $4 million. The moment they decide to keep the money, they become hostage to one another, and therefore damned—done in by a rats' nest of mistrust and deceit. As the born loser who feels the most guilt

(and therefore keeps tripping them up), Billy Bob Thornton proves, yet again, that he may be to stunted backwoods outcasts what Lon Chaney was to freaks.

6 **SLAM** The year's most overlooked—and misunderstood—movie. Telling the story of Ray (Saul Williams), a gentle-eyed poet-rapper from Washington, D.C., who gets busted on a minor marijuana charge, director Marc Levin, working in an electrifyingly precise documentary style, makes us feel the bureaucratic oppression of incarceration as no previous fiction feature has. The film was greeted as a sentimental outcry against a system that turns prisons into latter-day slave ships, but, in truth, it's about the complex intellectual journey Ray takes to *accept* his punishment. (To find freedom, he must embrace his chains.) Playing this

A Simple Plan

artist-naïf forced to grow into a man, Williams, as a presence, is tender, raging, and, in his spoken-word raps, symphonic.

7 **TWO GIRLS AND A GUY** Robert Downey Jr. has always been a wizardly enigma, a dervish joker riffing lightly in the void. But who is he, really? In James Toback's witty romantic-triangle talkathon, we finally get an answer. Downey plays Blake, a pathologically duplicitous actor who arrives at his Manhattan loft only to discover that his two "one and only" girlfriends (Heather Graham and Natasha Gregson Wagner) have found him out. The movie peels off Blake's deceptions one onion-skin layer at a time, but it's really meditating on the slippery identity of Downey himself—and on the spark of mystery at the heart of all relationships.

Slam

8 **BUFFALO 66** It's not unusual to see a star who's great at directing himself, but Vincent Gallo, in his filmmaking debut, parades—and deflates—his narcissism with arresting double vision. As the two-bit sociopath hero, who gets out of prison, kidnaps a jailbait cutie (Christina Ricci), and forces her to pretend to be his wife during a nightmarish visit home, Gallo is rude, hostile, punk-scraggly. As a filmmaker, he's clean, wise, heartfelt, as if he were staring at his own id and saying "What a jerk." *Buffalo 66* is the work of a powerful new voice, and it gives Ricci her best role to date: She says more here with one deadpan flirtatious glance than she does mouthing all the show-offy entendres of *The Opposite of Sex*.

9 **FOUR DAYS IN SEPTEMBER** Bruno Barreto's galvanic political docudrama is like *Z* replayed with riveting moral ambivalence. A cabal of middle-class Brazilian "revolutionaries" kidnap the U.S. ambassador (Alan Arkin) in Rio de Janeiro. On some level, the rebels are justified, but they're also fanatics. By dramatizing their actions from both sides, Barreto cuts through the usual liberal agitprop to lay bare the deeper tragedy of repressive regimes: the way they sow the seeds of fascism even in revolt.

10 **TOUCH OF EVIL** 1998 brought one of the great movies of 1958—Orson Welles' sleazo-gothic noir, an exhilarating fun house of corruption, paranoia, drugs, and dead-of-night chiaroscuro beauty. Now in the form that Welles intended, *Touch of Evil* is truly a new movie. It's shocking to see how many filmmakers were influenced by it (Hitchcock in *Psycho*, David Lynch in virtually every film he has made), or to realize that Welles, in his brilliant, lacerating performance as the bloated Hank Quinlan, foresaw his own flameout as surely as he imagined the future of cinema.

5 worst

1 **SIMON BIRCH** The retching essence of sentimental ick. It's the tale of a saintly junior dwarf who changes the lives of everyone around him, but even though we're supposed to "love" dear Simon, this dewy-eyed homuncular Christ is really just there to make us feel superior. The movie is like a Hallmark adaptation of one of those *National Enquirer* look-at-this-cute-little-deformed-person photos.

2 **MEN WITH GUNS** The talented but lethally self-serious John Sayles has made the ultimate politically correct dud. It's set in an unnamed Latin American country, it's about the victimization of peasant folk, it's filmed in Spanish and assorted Indian dialects (for that subtitled Peace Corps effect), and it's paced slower than a Robert Bresson film festival. I spent the entire movie wishing I were back in school.

3 **SNAKE EYES** The trash apotheosis of Brian De Palma. In this seriously deranged suspenser about the assassination of the U.S. secretary of defense during a championship boxing match (oh, *that* old plot!), not only does he reference *Vertigo*, the JFK assassination, and '70s conspiracy films—he references his own earlier rip-offs of same. The result is nearly metaphysical in its awfulness. We can't believe a minute of what we're seeing, but we certainly believe that Nicolas Cage, clad in a party-on jacket the color of dog puke, has come to think that *really* bad acting is good acting.

4 **BLADE** Wesley Snipes, as a fearless vampire killer, looks deader than the undead in this incoherent glitter-gore junk-athon. Please, no more movies based on comic books—they're about as appetizing as blood-filled Twinkies.

5 **FEAR AND LOATHING IN LAS VEGAS** Terry Gilliam adapted Hunter S. Thompson's hyperactive road-trip screed with more grunge, faithfulness, and madcap visual ingenuity than other filmmakers have lavished on the Bible or Dickens. The result? A movie that makes you wish Hunter S. Thompson had never picked up a typewriter.

vision

> by <

KEN TUCKER

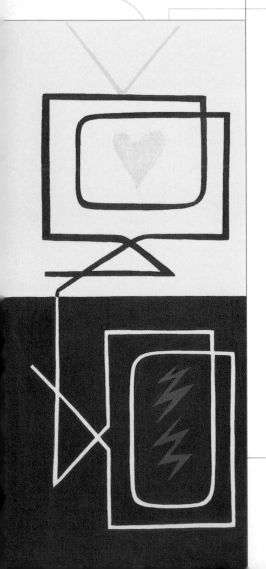

BUFFY THE VAMPIRE SLAYER *(The WB)*
Like people who hate hip-hop without listening to it, those who disdain *Buffy* without watching it are to be pitied for their closed minds. What fun they're missing with the only teen show that manages to work on many levels, nourishing even adult viewers. Most episodes in 1998 seized on a typical teen crisis—learning to drive, cramming for the SATs, running away from home after a fight with mom—and artfully turned it into a pretext for supernatural deviousness and martial-arts horror splatterings. For me, the season was all the better for the low profile kept by the series' most humorless character, Angel (David Boreanaz), during his near-death (near-life?) experience. The dizzying romantic quadrangle involving Xander (Nicholas Brendon), Willow (Alyson Hannigan), Oz (Seth Green), and Cordelia (Charisma Carpenter) is almost Shakespearean in its intricate wittiness. Indeed, the show has proved remarkably deft at deepening nearly every character's personality while maintaining a slapsticky, cartoonish exaggeration that yields much bloody laughter. Not only the year's best, but also the most underrated.

Buffy the Vampire Slayer

2 **THE LARRY SANDERS SHOW** *(HBO)* The series spent its final season pursuing an inevitable conclusion—the end of *The Larry Sanders Show*, with Larry (an ever more morose, dark-minded Garry Shandling) wallowing in his insecurities and self-absorption. The real-life drama surrounding Shandling and his seemingly quixotic split with longtime manager Brad Grey only injected additional where-does-the-show-end-and-reality-begin resonance into the series. Always willing to make a hilarious fool of himself so long as the fool remained tortured, Shandling turned Larry into a black hole of celebrity: Everyone from fake-out substi-

tute host Jon Stewart to Jim Carrey (doing a brilliant, Singing Defective turn in the finale) was drawn into the bleak Sanders universe. Oh, yeah: It was real funny, too.

3 **THE X-FILES** *(Fox)* It's now clear that this series transcends the expected (but still exceedingly pleasurable) Mulder-Scully byplay, and I'm not referring to its government conspiracy-alien story lines. Rather, creator Chris Carter knows a more fundamental truth: that work—what you choose to do with your life as a productive human being—is at once the ultimate pleasure and the ultimate torture. The best

The X-Files

moments last year (feature film included) occurred during M&S' skirmishes with FBI bureaucracy, but as often as not, these took place in non-conspiracy episodes, such as the recent Bermuda Triangle triumph.

4 FRIENDS *(NBC)* A minor miracle: While exec producers Marta Kauffman, David Crane, and Kevin Bright were busy presiding over the unfortunate artistic failure of *Jesse* and the ongoing disaster that is *Veronica's Closet, Friends* actually managed to get better, and it wasn't in any sort of creative slump to begin with. Just when I thought I'd had more than enough of the hangdog whine of Ross (David Schwimmer), the staff writers tossed him a fine bone to sink his teeth into: the abortive marriage with English prissy miss Emily (Helen Baxendale), which in turn gave Jennifer Aniston a chance to shine anew as a suddenly dumped Rachel. Add the apparently endless monkeyshines the writers can devise for roommates Chandler (Matthew Perry) and Joey (Matt LeBlanc), a revitalized intensity in the way Courteney Cox is attacking the role of Monica, and the truly touching surrogate pregnancy for Phoebe (Lisa Kudrow), and you've got the season's best ensemble work.

5 EVERYBODY LOVES RAYMOND *(CBS)* EW reader mail to the contrary, anyone who watches this sitcom regularly would realize that far from being on the producers' pad, I and my office colleagues shower *Raymond* with praise because it consistently takes the most threadbare, worn-out format known to television—the family sitcom—and pumps it up with laughing gas that doubles as truth serum. This season has benefited from beefing up the presence of once-beefy brother Robert (the svelte Brad Garrett), who flew from the nest of his mom and dad (that Möbius strip of bad parenting, Doris Roberts and Peter Boyle) only to crash, thuddingly, into the far greater problems of a single guy living alone.

6 THE PRACTICE *(ABC)* In the law universe according to writer-producer David E. Kelley, Bobby Donnell (stalwart Dylan McDermott) is as centered and sensible as Ally McBeal is flighty and foolish. This season, the series' strongest story arc involved defending a law professor (indispensable Über-WASP Edward Herrmann) against a murder charge, but it was the sidelights—things like giving Lara Flynn Boyle a more well-rounded personality, and introducing us to Bobby's janitor dad (Charles Durning)—that gave the show its soul.

7 SPORTS NIGHT *(ABC)* On a fictional third-place sports-news show, it's all wisecracks, all the time—except when it's all heartbreak. Creator Aaron Sorkin moved from feature films to a sitcom with a bold newcomer's sense of adventure, speeding up the dialogue to an unheard-of pace even while slowing the emotional content to syrup consistency. But it all went down just fine by me: It's the sitcom that gives romanticism a good name.

8 **THE CHRIS ROCK SHOW** *(HBO)* Rock keeps getting better by narrowing his focus (highly unusual for an artist whose audience is expanding). Instead of using his new clout to court white entertainers, Rock is concentrating on black issues, grilling people like American Civil Rights Institute chairman Ward Connerly on his anti–affirmative-action stance and ending up with brilliantly bristling interviews. His sketch comedy and filmed bits were sharper too, and his monologues continue to make profane common sense. More power to him.

9 **THE SIMPSONS** *(Fox)* I would contend that after 10 seasons, *The Simpsons'* streak as a great sociopolitical satire is now unequaled in television history. Year-end checklist: an all-time great Halloween edition; an unexpected increase in the colors we see in Homer's emotional palette (he fell giddily in love with a lobster); and Bart remaining at once crueler than any character in *South Park* while continuing to display feelings of guilt and remorse that distinguish him from his crude descendants. Plus, the episode in which Homer dreamed of himself as Yogi Bear and Bart as Boo Boo was chokingly hysterical.

10 **THAT '70S SHOW** *(Fox)* People who dismiss it as conventional don't recognize *That '70s Show* as a heightened (and, frequently, high-as-a-kite) version of the conventional '70s sitcom. Lead teens Topher Grace and Laura Prepon are, week after week, turning in the sort of nuanced, finely detailed adolescent-angst performances that the gang from *Dawson's Creek* never achieves outside of its J. Crew photo spreads. And I haven't read a single review that gives this series credit for its signature technical gimmick—the recurring 360-degree shots in which the camera pans around and each young cast member tops the previous one's punchline. It's a new form of laugh getter: the circle joke.

1 **COSTELLO** *(Fox)* As the star of the umpteenth revenge-of-the-working-class sitcom, Sue Costello was singularly charmless, surrounded by even less charming supporting characters and woefully bad writing. Gone; good riddance. But *Holding The Baby*, sitcom excreta frequently concerning the poor baby's excreta, was gone, then reappeared, on Fox's schedule. It is requested to PLEASE go away, and good riddance when it does. Bring on more cartoons.

2 **DATELINE NBC** *(NBC)* Its few hard-news stories tended to be about Clinton-Lewinsky, while the rest of the time, this five-times-a-week entertainment-programming eater filled its hours with shameless sob stories and limp softnews items about diets, all delivered with even softer news techniques like schmaltzy mood music and re-creations.

3 **NASH BRIDGES** *(CBS)* While *Homicide: Life on the Street* was in reruns, I finally decided to see what good old Don Johnson was up to. I was shocked—shocked!—to see that all he's doing is coasting and grinning along with pal Cheech Marin through a series of sub-*Matlock* crime plots. The final straw: introducing Yasmine Bleeth, swaddling her in dumpy clothes, and burying her natural likability.

4 **SUDDENLY SUSAN, CAROLINE IN THE CITY** *(NBC)* The end of feminism? Simone de Beauvoir died for their sins? Only if Sartre died for Conrad Bloom's.

5 **LEGACY** *(UPN)* An equine soap in which the horses display more emotion than any human. Marginally worse than NBC's *Wind on Water*, in which it was impossible to tell the buff, wooden actors from their gleaming surfboards.

Everybody Loves Raymond

Sports Night

> by <

DAVID BROWNE

THE MISEDUCATION OF LAURYN HILL / LAURYN HILL

(Ruffhouse/Columbia) While her cohorts in the Fugees made do with recycling other people's hits, Lauryn Hill opted for a different and far loftier goal: to create one of the most forceful statements ever by a woman in pop. With *The Miseducation of Lauryn Hill*, most of which she wrote and produced herself, the 23-year-old accomplished exactly that. Hill is one stern puppy, using her songs to lecture the music business, African-American men and women, even anyone who attempted to talk her out of having a child. But the music constantly resists her dourness. This is an album of dazzling, free-flowing eclecticism: The rap is lean and taut, the reggae sways like the coolest island breeze, and the love rhapsodies swoon, thanks to the funky elegance of her own multitracked harmonies. *The Miseducation of Lauryn Hill* is unflinchingly intense in every aspect, yet it's informed by a love of music, a love of the healing power of the human voice, and a sense of self-respect that transcends the clichés of hip-hop and contemporary R&B. (Miseducation? Compared with Hill, most of today's dressed-up divas sound like they should be the ones returning to school.) Even if you wouldn't want to be trapped next to Hill at a party, her first solo missive sets the standard for a new breed of pop. It's music without borders, a truly world beat.

music

Lauryn Hill

2 **"THE ROCKAFELLER SKANK" / FATBOY SLIM** *(Astralwerks, single)* It's official: Electronica is the next big thing of twisted-kicks singles. From Air's ooh-la-lull "Sexy Boy" to the Propellerheads' head rush "Bang On!" to the Crystal Method's diva-fueled "Comin' Back," techno-colored hits are flying around faster than hypocritical congressmen in Washington. The king of this particular hill is Fatboy Slim, the artist formerly known as British DJ Norman Cook. A piece of demented, speed-freak funk, "The Rockafeller Skank" hooks you in with its incessantly looped rap sample ("Check it out now/The funk soul brother"). But notice too how Cook continually alters the track's musical bed with each verse—from surf guitar to vocal chants to drum breaks to ringing telephones—and thereby tosses record-making conventions on their ear. Like the best of this genre, "The Rockafeller Skank" leaves you dazed, confused—and undeniably buzzed.

3 **THIS IS HARDCORE / PULP** *(Island)* Pulp headmaster Jarvis Cocker populates his latest songs with loners and losers desperately searching for physical or karmic satisfaction in an uptight world. It would be a seamy, disturbing listen—the equivalent to the movie *Happiness*—if it weren't for the music that drives and uplifts both Cocker's songs and his dry, cracked-actor delivery. Equal parts decadent cabaret, supper-club elegance, and blaring glam, *This Is Hardcore* places Pulp alongside David Bowie and the Kinks as twin-razor-edged mixers of music-hall theatricality and lordly rock. By the end, you're thankful that none of Cocker's characters are you—just as you're realizing that a little part of you resides in every one of them.

4 **UP / R.E.M.** *(Warner Bros.)* Here's how old-school R.E.M. are: For their all-eyes-on-them debut as a truncated trio, they make an album that requires time and patience, neither of which are valued qualities in today's hyperactive record biz. What at first seems like a rhythm-challenged, low-fi-techno murk gradually unfolds as a work of quiet beauty and dignity—electronic-folk-mass hymns without the church. Michael Stipe's voice has rarely sounded this supple, the band rarely this exploratory. As they grow older, quirkier, and more stubborn, R.E.M. ironically tap into the universal: sorrow, distance, regret, and, now and then, cautious optimism.

5 RAY OF LIGHT / **MADONNA** (Maverick) Is the sudden spirituality, the striking of the latest market-aware pose, easy to swallow? Of course not. Are the electronica baubles that producer William Orbit threads through these tranquilizing meditations occasionally corny? Sure enough. Does any of it make Madonna's techno-lite overhaul, its blend of insinuating hooks and automatic-brew throb, any less intoxicating? Not in the least.

6 "I'LL GO ON LOVING YOU" / **ALAN JACKSON** (Arista, single) Ever since country's early-'90s boom, Nashville ballads have become as slick and impersonal as sitcom theme songs—witness Shania Twain's "You're Still the One." Thank whichever Lord you like, then, for Jackson's neo-gothic paean to the "pleasures of the flesh." Those mournfully plucked guitar notes, those draping strings, that half-spoken, half-sung pillow-talk delivery—it's Barry White as Wichita lineman.

7 MECHANICAL ANIMALS / **MARILYN MANSON** (Nothing/Interscope) No, this isn't a typo. The rap-meets-hardcore melee of Korn and its ilk made the headlines, but in the world of hard rock, Manson made the album that withstands repeated plays. Creepy but funny, bludgeoning but unexpectedly melodic, heavily produced but with a long-overdue infusion of dynamics and nuked-city milieu, *Mechanical Animals* is the sound of a one-yuk band coming into its conceptual own. In a sorry year for rock, it's also a welcome reminder that alienated-adolescent lyrics, air-guitar-worthy hooks, and a dark-side-of-the-goon ambiance can still rock our world. I'm 18 again, and I like it.

R.E.M.

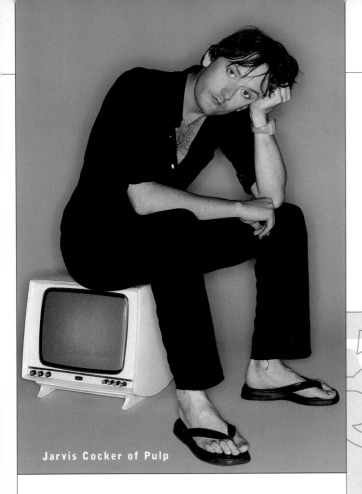

Jarvis Cocker of Pulp

10 **RED RICE / ELIZA CARTHY** *(Topic)* Posing with her fiddle on the inside cover, her lip pierced and hair punky red, British folkie Carthy is a vision of both 1998 and 1798. That's also true of this ambitious two-disc set—one contemporary-minded, the other traditional—on which Carthy threads jazz, dub bass, and techno with fiddle and accordion playing. Her singing, whether on a doleful folk ballad or Ben Harper's "Walk Away," is stoic and eloquent with an undercurrent of old-fashioned Celtic fatalism. Carthy competed against the Verve and Massive Attack for Britain's prestigious Mercury Music Prize, but *Red Rice* is more than just the year's darkest-horse nominee. It updates traditional music for the next century while retaining miles-deep roots. Hearing it is like visiting a newly refurbished British castle.

8 **RUFUS WAINWRIGHT / RUFUS WAINWRIGHT** *(DreamWorks)* Sean Lennon has the indie cred and Chris Stills the inherited sideburns, but when it comes to making resplendent music that owes nothing to famous rock forebears, Rufus Wainwright's got game. If anything, Wainwright owes more to Porter and Gershwin than to his acid-folk parents, Loudon Wainwright III and Kate McGarrigle. With its ballroom-dance orchestration and saloon pianos, the dreamily luxurious *Rufus Wainwright* has the feel of a lost weekend at the Algonquin Hotel. Yet unlike the cloying swing-music revival, Wainwright's music is thoroughly modern, from its subtly gay sensibility to its wary romanticism. "You will believe in love and all it's supposed to be," he sings, "but just until the fish start to smell." Maybe, but right now, *Rufus Wainwright* smells like nothing less than the start of an auspicious career.

9 **LIVE 1966: THE BOOTLEG SERIES VOL. 4 (THE "ROYAL ALBERT HALL" CONCERT) / BOB DYLAN** *(Columbia/Legacy)* Capturing the period in the Bard's career when he veered from folk to rock and literally amplified his songs, this long-bootlegged, three-decade-old live tape is undeniable history. But for once in the boxed-set era, it's history of the least musty, most stirring sort. The acoustic tracks on the first disc have a timeless, lyrical beauty (the same goes for that voice), while the hair-tugging, full-metallic racket on disc 2—complete with scattered boos from the discombobulated British audience—hasn't lost any of its barbed-wire spikiness. Imagine that: a pop artist deliberately confounding his audience. Thirty-two years on, both music and lesson continue to resound.

worst

1 **BEFORE THESE CROWDED STREETS / DAVE MATTHEWS BAND** *(RCA)* Labored singing, self-righteous political commentary, dippy ballads, way too many woodwind solos—Jethro Tull were filling stadiums once upon a time too.

2 **VAN HALEN 3 / VAN HALEN** *(Warner Bros.)* Which were more grueling: the painfully grizzled thumpings this band now makes, or new lead singer Gary Cherone's painful attempts to sound grizzled? Somewhere, David Lee Roth is laughing even louder than he normally does.

3 **MP DA LAST DON / MASTER P** *(No Limit/Priority)* It's hard to say which of this year's 652 assembly-line No Limit releases is the worst, so let's put the onus on the master of the whole dreary enterprise. As impressive as P's entrepreneurial skills may be, *MP Da Last Don* is two dreary discs of gangsta clichés, nonexistent tunes, and bargain-basement production. Questionable innovation: Guest Snoop Dogg coins the term "niggette."

4 **ALL SAINTS / ALL SAINTS** *(London)* Yes, they can harmonize in key, unlike the Spice Girls. And yes, as they repeatedly informed us, they can also compose their own songs, unlike the former fab five. But when said harmonies and songwriting are as drab and lifeless as this debut, all the declarations amount to naught. The year's dullest party.

5 **CELEBRITY SKIN / HOLE** *(DGC)* From crass soundtracks to numerous Backstreet Boys knockoffs, hundreds of worse albums were released this year. But in terms of crushed expectations, Courtney Love's spiritless return to rock eclipses them all. Her voice flat and grating, the potentially poppy melodies weighted down by ill-placed rock crunch, *Celebrity Skin* is as much work to listen to as it reportedly was to make.

books

A MAN IN FULL / TOM WOLFE

(Farrar, Straus & Giroux, $28.95) In a world woefully overstocked with timid literary miniatures and pallid, slender tales, this novel is a Lincoln Continental, an Eiffel Tower—nay, an Everest. Its author, perhaps our last robust maximalist, picks up the preoccupations of 1987's *The Bonfire of the Vanities*—race relations, class, power, status, sex, and, most of all, money—and runs with them all the way into the millennial end zone. A spectacularly observed, ruthlessly sardonic 742 pages, *A Man in Full* is the story of two men: a nouveau riche real estate mogul named Charlie Croker who's descended deep into debt, and a hyper-assimilated, disdainful African-American lawyer named Roger White II. Sure, some readers may object to the ferocity of Wolfe's racially charged satire, but no one is spared his scathing commentary. There are but a few novelists who even try to cover this much of the American canvas, fewer still whose brushstrokes are so sweeping and yet so precise. Grand and glorious entertainment from one of our national treasures.

2 **BRIDGET JONES'S DIARY / HELEN FIELDING** *(Viking, $22.95)* A few critics dismissed it as a trivial daily catalog of one woman's weight, alcohol intake, cigarette use, and love life, but we suspect they were just jealous. This subversive, verbally astute British import inspired a hundred inferior imitators, perked up a wan postfeminist national dialogue, kicked Ally McBeal's nonexistent derriere, and, most important, made us laugh uproariously at ourselves and each other. All in all, it was a v.v. good year.

3 **EASY RIDERS, RAGING BULLS: HOW THE SEX-DRUGS-AND-ROCK 'N' ROLL GENERATION SAVED HOLLYWOOD / PETER BISKIND** *(Simon & Schuster, $25)* A scathing history of how the finest directors of a fine film decade—the 1970s—had it and then lost it. With Robert Altman, Francis Ford Coppola, Peter Bogdanovich, and a cast of coke-snorting, backstabbing hundreds, this scrupulously researched account is salty with flavorsome gossip, sour with the aftertaste of misspent careers, intoxicating with one revelation after another, and bitter with decades-old grudges. But the flourish of this dish of a book is that its author cares so much about what went right: the movies.

4 **KAATERSKILL FALLS / ALLEGRA GOODMAN** *(Dial, $23.95)* The wise-beyond-her-years Goodman, who refined her craft the old-fashioned way (wonderful, warm short stories), has come of age. This, her first novel, portrays an insular group of Orthodox Jews who summer in the upstate New York town of the title. During the Bicentennial, they hoist small flags of independence: A rabbi befriends a rebel-

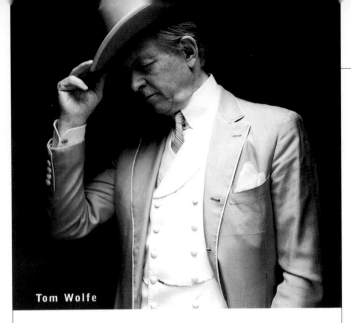

Tom Wolfe

lious Syrian neighbor; a mother opens a grocery store. It's a quiet celebration of the American dream.

5 **FREEDOMLAND / RICHARD PRICE** (Broadway, $25) We're back in fictitious Dempsy, N.J., the setting for Price's 1992 *Clockers*, and the vibe is just as grim. Brenda Martin, a white woman, claims that her son was kidnapped by an African American; there's a weary tough-love cop, a cynical street reporter, and a group of zealous child finders on the case. This psychically draining work of fiction presents an unflinching view of our nation's race relations.

6 **THE FARMING OF BONES / EDWIDGE DANTICAT** (Soho, $23) A doomed fictional love affair between a domestic servant and a sugarcane cutter is skillfully grafted onto a tragic episode of Haitian history: the 1937 massacre of civilians by the Dominican army. In depicting the struggle over a shared homeland, Danticat (recent Oprah anointee for *Breath, Eyes, Memory*) deploys a rich prose arsenal and a sensitive grasp of complex material. Rarely has the literature of loss and oppression been rendered with such clear-eyed, painstaking economy.

7 **ECOLOGY OF FEAR / MIKE DAVIS** (Metropolitan, $27.50) A tonic for anyone under the misapprehension that Los Angeles is crawling with glamorous movie stars...when in fact it's crawling with killer bees, rats, and mountain lions against a lovely backdrop of fire, riots, droughts, earthquakes, and the occasional tornado. Davis' environmentally oriented follow-up to his social analysis of the world's most blisteringly tawdry megalopolis (*City of Quartz*) is a similarly attuned piece of class and racial reportage, a trenchant tale of rich people hunkering down behind their privet hedges and masses looting roach spray.

8 **RESERVATION ROAD / JOHN BURNHAM SCHWARTZ** (Knopf, $24) This second novel is one of the rare instances when prepublication buzz actually meant something. Ten-year-old Josh Learner is killed by a hit-and-run driver, an almost alcoholic named Dwight Arno with a 10-year-old son of his own. The book's obvious villain emerges as its most fascinating figure, and his inevitable showdown with the victim's father throbs with suspense and moral ambiguity. One of the most unflinching evocations of an ordinary family coping with despair since *Ordinary People*.

9 **THE POISONWOOD BIBLE / BARBARA KINGSOLVER** (HarperFlamingo, $26) Kingsolver most readily conjures up the Southwest (*The Bean Trees, Animal Dreams*), but here the biologist with an eye for detail transposes her talents to a Belgian Congo brimming with tropical flowers and venomous snakes. There, a Baptist missionary family is the de facto exotic species, but its story—narrated by the holy man's wife and four daughters over 40 years—is just as much about a region struggling with colonial legacies as it is about intergenerational dynamics. A timely, complex novel that's lush with stylistic marvels.

10 **THE AMAZING "TRUE" STORY OF A TEENAGE SINGLE MOM / KATHERINE ARNOLDI** (Hyperion, $16) A comic book in the top 10? Ah, but this is hardly your average comic book, and Arnoldi is hardly your average superheroine: raped and left pregnant at 17; drummed down into dead-end, hazardous jobs; shunned by her family. Not only did she beat back a grim fate, but the bright, redemptive way she shares her story is proof that one evocative line drawing can be worth a thousand points of psychobabble. If you're looking for a good, cleansing cry—and a book that makes you think about the world instead of just escaping it—this is the best bet.

1 **MESSAGE IN A BOTTLE / NICHOLAS SPARKS** (Warner, $20) Ms. Lewinsky's a fan, but we beg to differ: *The Starr Report* is a lot juicier than this leaden, platitudinous story about a mirthless newspaper columnist and a bereft widower who pursue an interminable long-distance relationship. The only message we could divine? This book...sinks.

2 **THE VAMPIRE ARMAND / ANNE RICE** (Knopf, $26.95) Rice is ripe for a makeover. This monstrous mishmash begins with a grotesquely florid account of the protagonist's early years in Venice, segues into graphic descriptions of his sexual awakening, and then takes off into truly hokey liturgy. Net effect: a writer who at this point isn't even sure which of her own books she's plagiarizing.

3 **BELLADONNA / KAREN MOLINE** (Warner, $25) If ever a novel was conceived as a marketing exercise, it's this overwrought ghost story, bought for $1 million and launched with its own tie-in fragrance. Alas, nothing could sweeten Moline's tiresome plot (Italian spas, twin brothers, revenge), which is so loopy and twisted, it's difficult to tell one decade from the next.

4 **ALL THE LEONARDO DiCAPRIO QUICKIE BIOS / ASSORTED OFFENDERS** A recycled quote here. A perky quizlet there. A generous smattering of photographs. Nope, nothing—not even a judicious sprinkling of the dulcet phrase "piercing blue eyes"—can make these look-alike albums anything more than the pathetic clip jobs they are.

5 **SPICE WORLD / THE SPICE GIRLS** (Three Rivers Press, $15) This tired tie-in has all the zest of rejected cover-album art (which it could well be); to add insult to idiocy, it seems to have entirely escaped the copy editing process.

video

> by <

TY BURR

KIKI'S DELIVERY SERVICE *(Buena Vista, G)* In a year in which the animation breakthroughs on the big screen involved computers and bugs (no, not that kind), the video that gave me the purest home-viewing enjoyment was a cartoon about a sweet-faced adolescent witch. Made in 1989. *Hand drawn*. Animator Hayao Miyazaki has been called "the Walt Disney of Japan," and, ironically, it's Walt Disney that is finally releasing his films in this country, with celeb-studded English language tracks. Still, even as the characters speak in the familiar cadences of Janeane Garofalo and the late Phil Hartman, *Kiki* remains a beguiling fever dream of childlike nostalgia. On one level, it's as archetypal as a Joseph Campbell myth: Thirteen-year-old Kiki (Kirsten Dunst) leaves her parents to find her place in the world, ultimately settling on a coastal city that Miyazaki envisions as being in a 1950s Europe where WWII never happened. In another sense, it's a deeply reassuring parable of belonging. And on the visual level, it's simply astounding, like one of Hergé's Tintin landscapes unstuck in time, or a *Little Nemo in Speed Racer Land*. Next year Miyazaki's '97 hit *Princess Mononoke* will be released in U.S. theaters. For now, *Kiki* serves as a reminder in these antsy times that the best animated films are never about how the dots connect, but where they take you.

2 **STARSHIP TROOPERS** *(Columbia TriStar, R)* Neo-fascist tripe aimed at the empty space between the ears of MTV-addled teenagers? A fiendishly encoded critique of our cultural tastes? Or just a genetically superior bugs-from-outer-space flick? At least half the fun of Paul Verhoeven's future-schlock epic lies in trying to figure out his intentions. There's no one answer, either: This director is the kind of tricky bastard who'll throw Neil Patrick Harris *(Doogie Howser, M.D.)* in an SS trench coat, call him a good guy, then let you stew over your own response. Forget Gus Van Sant's *Psycho—this* is the postmodern Hollywood art film of the year.

3 **LES VAMPIRES/IRMA VEP** *(Water Bearer, unrated/Fox Lorber, unrated)* Maids and aristocrats, office workers and policemen: In Louis Feuillade's gloriously surreal 1915–16 serial, the members of the criminal gang known as the Vampires are everywhere and everyone. It's the first intimation of

's Delivery
ice

the Pod People, the first filmed expression of 20th-century paranoia, and as modern as *The X-Files*. At the center of the madness is the incredible Musidora as arch-vamp Irma Vep, who's also the oblique subject of Olivier Assayas' *Irma Vep*, a bitterly funny after-dinner mint to *Les Vampires* about a hapless director (Jean-Pierre Léaud) trying to remake the silent classic for the 1990s. *Vampires* shows French cinema literally being born; 80 years later, *Irma Vep* caustically presides over its funeral.

4 **EYE OF GOD** (*Peachtree, R*) A small, still slice of American pie, Tim Blake Nelson's debut skirts art-house/heartland pretensions to end up as a translucently moving vision of faith and bad luck. An Oklahoma burger waitress (Martha Plimpton) marries the born-again ex-con (Kevin Anderson) to whom she's been writing and—so gradually that it's almost invisible—Mr. Right turns into Mr. Righteous. Meanwhile, a mournful teen rebel (Nick Stahl) aimlessly drives the back roads by night, spiraling in toward their conjoined fates. Like an infinitely sympathetic surgeon, Nelson intercuts between past, near past, and present, circling around a hideous act of violence until we can no longer look away—and then slips us a scene of overpowering grace in its place.

5 **EASY LIVING** (*Universal, unrated*) Why has this sidesplitting 1937 entry in the Preston Sturges canon been unavailable on video until this year? Perhaps because Sturges only wrote the script, while the witty, sophisticated, criminally neglected Mitchell Leisen directed it. No matter: *Easy Living*'s a scream from the moment that fur coat falls on Jean Arthur's head as she rides a double-decker bus down Fifth Avenue. Its merciless satire of Wall Street's lemming mentality makes even more sense in these days of Internet IPOs, and Sturges freaks, take note: It was Leisen who concocted the Automat riot that is the film's slapstick high point. All the more reason for Universal to get off its butt and release such Leisen classics as *Arise, My Love* and *Hold Back the Dawn*.

6 **A PERSONAL JOURNEY WITH MARTIN SCORSESE THROUGH AMERICAN MOVIES** (*Miramax, unrated*) Scratch any filmmaker (or film critic) and you'll find a kid pale from sitting in darkened movie theaters, trembling with discovery. Martin Scorsese, bless him, is still in daily contact with that kid, so his nearly four-hour tour plays like a clip-happy lecture series given by your best friend from college.

Produced for and originally aired on British TV in 1995, *Journey* focuses on tormented geniuses (Nicholas Ray, Orson Welles) at the expense of comic geniuses (Howard Hawks, W.C. Fields), but that's to be expected for a man who himself is a querulous industry outsider.

7 **THE KILLERS** (*Universal, unrated*) Previous movies may have lined up the pieces of film noir, but this hard-hearted 1946 thriller added the miracle ingredient of post-WWII despair and arguably stands as the first perfect example of the genre. Expanding on an Ernest Hemingway short story, director Robert Siodmak creates a shadowy, ulcerated view of American life where no friendship is safe from the double cross and where no woman—*especially* not Ava Gardner—is who she seems. Burt Lancaster made his film debut as the doomed Swede, and it's startling to see the actor's rueful, bottled-up machismo already fully formed.

8 **L.A. CONFIDENTIAL** (*Warner, R*) Want to convert hesitant friends to the wonders of DVD? Invite them over to sample the best film of 1997 (you heard me, and no arguments) in the format it deserves. You get your wide-screen imagery in crystalline detail—but you also get behind-the-scenes swag that includes an interactive map of L.A. highlighting historical locations, director Curtis Hanson re-creating the "photo pitch" by which he sold the studio on the film, and (drooler alert!) a no-dialogue version of the film featuring only the music track's pop songs and Jerry Goldsmith's score. Oh, and you get a film with richer characters, better plotting, and more interesting notions about loyalty than anything else released in 1998.

9 **THE BIG LEBOWSKI** (*PolyGram, R*) All those critics who gushed over *Fargo* grew stiff with dismay at the Coen brothers' follow-up, and, yes, the movie *is* something equivalent to passing gas in an art-house cinema. But, hey, why *shouldn't* intellectuals have their very own *There's Something About Mary*? Especially when this one delivers Jeff Bridges as a contentedly faded hippie enmeshed in a kidnapping case, a vicious ferret in the bathtub, John Goodman as an Orthodox Jewish bowling freak, John Turturro in a skintight purple jumpsuit, and everyone from Booker T. & the M.G.'s to Yma Sumac on the soundtrack? Think Steely Dan making a film noir and you're almost there.

10 **THE GRAND JURY TESTIMONY OF WILLIAM JEFFERSON CLINTON** (*MPI, unrated*) Because its total absence of meaningful content said everything (or nothing) about what the President did (or didn't) do, and about what Kenneth Starr's real agenda is (or isn't). Because, unlike a website, the video is a physical object that can be passed down for generations as documentation of a profoundly stupid moment in our country's history. Because the tape, along with Bill Gates' testimony to the Department of Justice, reveals that official double-talk has arrived at Orwellian purity only 14 years behind schedule. Because we get the entertainment and the politicians we deserve. And because there is no longer any difference.

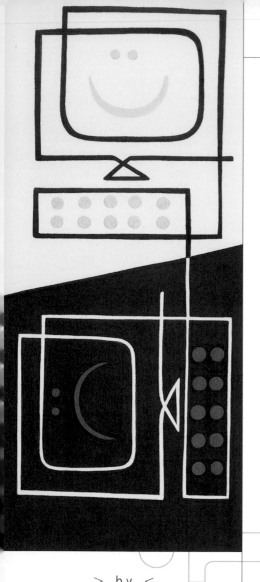

> by <

**TY BURR AND
GARY ENG WALK**

STAR WARS: BEHIND THE MAGIC

(LucasArts, CD-ROM for PC, $29.95) Stormtroopers are superb tap dancers. That's just one of a jillion epiphanies we experienced in this brilliantly executed reference CD-ROM—the ultimate guide to all things *Star Wars* and one of the few worthy multimedia adjuncts to a Hollywood property. The two-disc set pools the vast universe of *Star Wars* movies (including a peek at gizmos and characters from *Star Wars: Episode I—The Phantom Menace*), novels, comic books, games, toys, and documentaries—and somehow presents the morass in an organized, vastly entertaining on-screen encyclopedia. Each click of the mouse reveals another gem, from the simple (an animated, beeping R2-D2 that introduces a video clip) to the outrageously grandiose (the lighthearted Weapons Test Facility that demonstrates the relative powers of blasters, lightsabers, even the Death Star cannon by firing on one unlucky stormtrooper). With *Star Wars* mania once again at a fever pitch, isn't it nice to have a real scorecard to what happened a long, long time ago in that galaxy far, far away?

2 **E! ONLINE** *(www.eonline.com)* With the glut of entertainment-news websites out there—*Entertainment Asylum, Mr. Showbiz,* our own damn fine EW ONLINE—it might seem hard for any one of them to leave a lasting impression. Yet the E! Entertainment cable channel's online outpost keeps us browsing day after day, week after week. What's the secret? Tons of *stuff:* A-list celebrity chats, gossip, reams of factoids, reviews, links up the ying-yang, wry interactive games like "Studio Boss," Marilyn Beck, a shopping mall—and it's all pulled together through a frothy interface and a consistent, deeply wisenheimer tone. The result is one of the handful of Web properties that actually improve on their source.

3 **MP3** *(www.mp3.com)* It seems 1998 was the year in which all those kids up to no good in their bedrooms and college dorms—downloading and playing (gasp!) often-illegal music files—finally caught the eye of the music industry, which shrieked in dismay, asked the government to outlaw a new Walkman-style player that would let you take those tunes off your computer and carry them around, and sputtered in disbelief when a federal judge said no. We may see this one in court in '99; but for now, getting your music via the Net has arrived, and MP3 is far and away the populist format of choice. Will it transform the industry? Maybe not—but we'd hate to own a record store in five years.

media

4 **METAL GEAR SOLID** (*Konami, for PlayStation, $50*) The videogame industry saw its own Event Movie in 1998, and unlike the Hollywood variety (hello, *Godzilla*), the real thing actually surpassed the pre-release hype. *Metal Gear* puts you in control of macho government agent Solid Snake as he battles a megalomaniac with a nuclear weapon that's invisible to all radar (uh-oh!). The action is literally heart pounding: At times the game simulates your pulse racing by signaling your force-feedback joystick to thump. But most welcome is that rarest of features in games—and movies—nowadays: careful attention to plot and character development.

5 **SALON MAGAZINE** (*www.salonmag.com*) The San Francisco-based online journal has been winning best-of-the-Web awards since its 1995 launch, but 1998 finally saw it entering the mainstream discourse—albeit controversially, with painstaking investigations of Kenneth Starr and the revelation, in September, of Rep. Henry Hyde's adulterous affair of 30 years ago (*Salon*'s Washington bureau chief, Jonathan Broder, argued against running that story and resigned shortly thereafter). Infamy aside, the magazine continues to publish thoughtful, beautifully written pieces on everything under the sun, making it one of the Net's few genuine must-reads.

6 **THE iMac** About the only thing it didn't win was the Nobel Peace Prize. In its brief lifetime, Apple's wonder box—a curvaceous, 38-pound, translucent blue-and-white computer—has saved the company from public and financial oblivion (it's no coincidence that Apple enjoyed its first profit in three fiscal years), earned design and technical awards from the media, and spawned the kind of fan websites usually reserved for Jennifer Love Hewitt. The celebrity status is well deserved: It's loaded with a lusty G3 processor and all of the trimmings, and users can set up the machine and get online in minutes, all for $1,299. Kind of makes you wonder why no other computer maker can think this different.

7 **THE LEGEND OF ZELDA: OCARINA OF TIME** (*Nintendo, for Nintendo 64, $69.95*) Nintendo 64's lack of killer apps—there hasn't been a monster hit since *Super Mario 64* two years ago—came to a momentous halt with the late-November arrival of *Zelda*, a fantasy-adventure game from the wildly imaginative mind of superstar game designer Shigeru Miyamoto. As the swashbuckling Link, a lad who's equal parts Peter Pan, Robin Hood, and Keebler elf, you explore an enchanting realm painted in the most ornate visuals you've ever seen in a videogame. And in a stunning redefinition of immersive gameplay, virtual days pass—marked by sunrises and sunsets and your character aging from boy to man—as you progress through the game. Serene and hypnotic, noble and beautiful, *Zelda*'s an instant classic.

8 **GAME BOY CAMERA** (*Nintendo, $49.95*) The resolution stinks. The screen's too small. And—somebody call the folks in Pleasantville!—the images are in black and white. Yet despite all of the shortcomings, there's something undeniably cool about making a camera out of the same Game Boy that's been around for nearly a decade—if only because it makes us feel like we're MacGyver. Available in a rainbow of colors and ingeniously simple to use (just plug the bug-eyed widget into the cartridge slot and shoot away; plug in the optional printer to put your photos on stickers), the camera is digital photography's poster boy for chic kitsch.

9 **ICQ** (*www.icq.com*) In reality, it's just a little window that sits on your computer screen and lets you know when any of your friends, anywhere around the world, are online and available to gab. In effect, this invention by four Israeli twentysomethings has turned the entire Internet into a cozy proprietary chat service. Launched in 1996, ICQ (I Seek You, get it?) achieved critical mass in 1998, with more than 20 million registered users by late October, must-have status among teenagers and college kids—and $287 million in the kitty when AOL snapped up parent company Mirabilis in June.

10 **PAUL IS DEAD.COM** (*www.paulisdead.com*) This splendidly rude Web serial was originally produced for the Microsoft Network—but who would have seen it there? Thankfully, Gates pulled the plug on MSN's entertainment shows, so West Coast-based virtual studio LaFong took its witty rock-paranoia tale to the greater Web. So who *did* kill Paul Lomo, tormented leader of the (fictional) early-'80s cult band Miasma? Our money's on Seneca, the Satan-worshipping lesbian bass player, but whoever dunnit, navigating the fake crazed-fan pages, audio snippets, mini-movies, and between-the-tracks "clues" remains fine, nasty fun.

Virtual Princess Leia

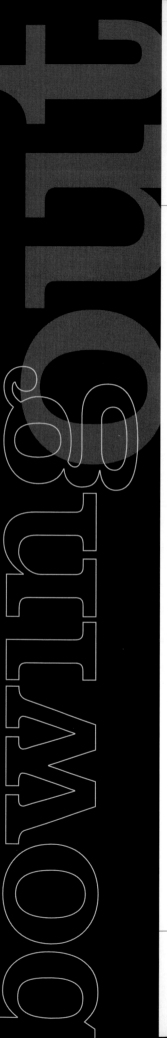

FRANK SINATRA | born 1915

FORGET THE RAT PACK. Those rambunctious antics with a gaggle of middle-aged adolescents, men all more modestly talented than himself, were always a front. Forget Ava and Mia and the starlets and showgirls; for all their beauty and provocation, they are mere footnotes in the artist's life. Forget the connections to Jack Kennedy and Sam Giancana; they are as inessential to the main thrust of his story as he is to theirs. Forget the movies: You already mostly have. Forget the pathologies and the uglinesses; forget the extraordinary generosity and deep, if apparently conditional, devotion—however God has held him accountable, we cannot measure him as we would a man of normal gifts. Forget everything but the voice, the voice, the voice. • Eons from now, when historians or anthropologists seek insight into mid-century America, they will find it essential to listen to the albums of Frank Sinatra. They will find it essential, for nowhere will they find better expressed the dreams of that generation of men—and it was men; Sinatra spoke to women, but he spoke *for* men—who, having survived the Depression and having won a world war, were then taking hold of the prime of their lives. Frank Sinatra gave voice to the emotional lives of those men. It's a quarter to three, he would sing, and there wouldn't be anybody who couldn't relate to what it was like to have outlasted everyone and everything but loneliness. That's life, he would sing, his attitude as brassy as the accompaniment, and no one who had ridden high in April and been shot down in May didn't feel the rueful exhilaration, the sheer kick that comes from rolling with the punches and hanging in. Come fly with me, he'd sing, I've got you under my skin, he'd sing, just the way you look tonight, he'd sing, and there would be captured in his voice the incandescent moment when love first appears and presents the possibility that everything from horizon to horizon will be all right. "High Hopes" and "The Best Is Yet to Come," he sang at one point; and then later it was "Here's to the Losers," "There Used to Be a Ballpark," "Send in the Clowns": The brash confidence of summer gave way to the philosophical assessments of the fall. • It's unfortunate that the monument of his later career is so often seen as the defensive, almost self-pitying "My Way," recorded in the late '60s when the WWII generation felt so assaulted. A far better valediction is his reading of "New York, New York." It's up to you, he sings, knowing that he had seen it all and done it all and felt it all, and if the listener chose to ignore him, well, who'd be the loser then? The straw-behind-the-ears lyrics of an eager youth turned into the triumphant, kick-down-the-doors, here-I-am song of a man in full. Forget all that tin-pot Chairman of the Board stuff. Remember how his singing makes you feel. —JAMIE MALANOWSKI

PHIL HARTMAN | born 1948

PHIL HARTMAN LIKED TO DESCRIBE HIMSELF as a "team player." His finest work did come in ensemble settings—as an indispensable cast member on *Saturday Night Live* from 1986 to 1994 and as the unctuous anchorman Bill McNeal on the NBC sitcom *NewsRadio* from 1995 to 1998. • But what Hartman was too humble to admit was that he was a team all by himself. On *SNL*, he impersonated everyone from Frank Sinatra to Frankenstein; his malleable features seemed to shift before our eyes. He was a master mimic as well: On *The Simpsons*, he gave voice to a panoply of Springfield residents, among them washed-up thespian Troy McClure and fly-by-night shyster Lionel Hutz. A low-key family man who had enjoyed an earlier career as a graphic artist (he designed album covers for Poco, America, and Crosby, Stills and Nash), Hartman suffered an unexpectedly sordid death—he was shot by his wife, Brynn, who then committed suicide. Yet long after the lurid details of his end have faded from our minds, Hartman's legacy of comedic virtuosity will live on. • Even though filmmakers never figured out how to harness the man's genius, wasting him in junk like *Greedy* and *Houseguest*, Hartman was comfortable with his level of fame. "My fans usually come up and say, 'Hey, I really like your work,'" he told EW in 1995. "They're not trying to rip my clothes off, but they want me to know that I make them laugh. Well, that just makes me feel great." The feeling was mutual. —BRUCE FRETTS

LINDA MCCARTNEY | born 1942

WE FIRST HEARD LINDA EASTMAN'S NAME in 1969, when she lived the dream of women everywhere and married "cute" Beatle Paul McCartney. Sharing the blame with Yoko Ono for breaking up the best-loved rock group in the world, Linda saw her popularity sink even further when McCartney insisted that she add her weak vocals to his new musical ensemble, Wings. ("I get a lot of flak from Paul, too," Linda once said. "He's on my case all the time.") But if her musical talents were questionable, her flair for photography was stunningly evident: Evocative pictures of Jimi Hendrix, the Doors, Bob Dylan, the Grateful Dead, and, of course, the Fab Four established her as a leading chronicler of the times. Still, Linda's most lasting gift may have been to inspire one of the century's great songwriters. "Any love song I write," Paul said in 1997, "is written for Linda." He adored her so much that during their 29-year marriage, the pair spent only 11 nights apart. In the time they were together, Linda carved out a reputation as an activist (on animal rights issues), a shrewd businesswoman (her meatless frozen-foods business was worth more than $30 million), and a fighter (she never surrendered to the breast cancer that was diagnosed in 1995). But on April 17, the woman for whom Paul McCartney wrote the words "Maybe I'm amazed at the way you love me all the time" died as she had lived: with her husband by her side. —CAREN WEINER CAMPBELL

AKIRA KUROSAWA | born 1910

THEY CALLED HIM "THE EMPEROR," and for good reason: A temperamental perfectionist, director Akira Kurosawa spent more than five decades lording it over cast and crew (he once ordered a medieval set rebuilt because a single nail head was visible). And the 25 movies he made from 1943 to 1993 were equally majestic. Kurosawa's East-meets-West style blended Japanese folklore and occidental filmmaking; "the Western and the Japanese live side by side in my mind naturally," he once said. In Kurosawa's hands, even Shakespeare spoke Japanese: *Macbeth* became 1957's terrifying *Throne of Blood*, *King Lear* 1985's operatic *Ran*. Kurosawa, who was inspired by the films of John Ford, saw his own films remade as American Westerns: 1954's *The Seven Samurai* morphed into 1960's *The Magnificent Seven*, and 1960's *Yojimbo* reappeared in 1964 as *A Fistful of Dollars*. Most memorably, Kurosawa's 1958 film *Hidden Fortress*, in which two argumentative peasants escort an endangered princess to safety, strongly influenced George Lucas' *Star Wars*—with the drones transformed into droids. But for all the recognition (he won Oscars for *Rashomon* in 1951 and for *Dersu Uzala* in 1976, as well as a 1990 Lifetime Achievement award from the Academy), the emperor remained humble: "When I am lucky," he once said, "the stories have a lifelike quality that makes them appealing to people." —CWC

JEROME ROBBINS | born 1918

"WHEN YOU'RE WORKING WITH HIM, it's hard to get out of bed in the morning—the challenge is so great, the labor is so difficult—but you do," Chita Rivera once said of Jerome Robbins, the theatrical genius who died of a stroke at age 79 on July 29. Robbins—a taskmaster whose brilliant fusion of Broadway's jazzy dance slang with the rarefied world of ballet earned him two Oscars (one honorary), five Tonys, and an Emmy over his 60-year career—inspired both reverence and fear. Dancers "didn't always like him," recalled Robert Wise, Robbins' codirector on the movie *West Side Story*, "but they respected him." ● It's not hard to see why. So prolific and inventive was Robbins that his list of credits reads like a roster of Broadway's greatest hits: *On the Town. Gypsy. The King and I. Peter Pan. Fiddler on the Roof.* "I rebel violently against being classified," he once said. This master of crossing boundaries, who brought ballet to the man on the street, also brought theater's unpretentious energy to classical dance. In the process, he almost single-handedly invented American choreography and enjoyed a career in ballet that was every bit as distinguished as (if less widely known than) his work in film and theater. ● "I am a perfectionist," Robbins once admitted. "I think that's what art is about—trying to make it as good as you possibly can."

SONNY BONO | born 1935

IT'S FITTING THAT ONE OF HIS EARLY HITS was called "Laugh at Me," because Sonny Bono built his career, both in showbiz and in politics, on self-effacing humor. As a young music producer, he "discovered" the teenage Cher in a coffee shop; when she proved too scared to perform alone, he joined her on stage, offsetting her jitters with his own loopy persona. A string of innocently groovy hits ("I Got You Babe," "The Beat Goes On") made the duo AM-radio fixtures in the late '60s and landed them a popular TV variety series. After the show—and their marriage—ended, Bono tried his hand at being a restaurateur. When a fracas over local zoning issues led him to run for mayor of Palm Springs, Calif., people laughed at the notion of a washed-up TV personality as chief executive. But Bono won handily and went on to a career as a U.S. congressman. (Even among fellow House members he played the clown, once ordering 15 pizzas during a gridlocked Judiciary Committee hearing.) When Bono died in a Nevada ski accident at age 62, Cher mourned publicly—"Son" clearly meant more to her than she'd realized. Bono's imprint on pop culture may be similar. Like Cher, few of us knew how much we'd miss him until he was gone. —JOE NEUMAIER

ALAN J. PAKULA | born 1928

ALAN J. PAKULA ONCE SAID THAT WHAT INTERESTED HIM was "a man who is in control, and inside there is a frightened child." And Pakula, who at one point considered a career in psychiatry, brought that edgy introspection to each of his films. Perhaps best known for his paranoid trilogy—*Klute*, *The Parallax View*, and *All the President's Men*—Pakula was a master of movies that raised troubling questions without necessarily offering answers. He began his career producing *To Kill a Mockingbird*, and when he died on Nov. 19 at age 70 in a car crash, he was working on a script about Franklin and Eleanor Roosevelt. About what drew him to serious subjects at a time when Hollywood was increasingly taken with the inconsequential, Pakula once said, "Draw your own conclusions." —MATTHEW MCCANN FENTON

ROY ROGERS & GENE AUTRY | born 1911 and 1907

"AN INTROVERT AT HEART" is how Roy Rogers described himself. His friendly rival for title of King of the Cowboys, Gene Autry, was similarly self-effacing: "My friends kidded me about going so far on such modest talent," he said, "and I always agreed with them." Don't be fooled. The two defined honor and masculine virtue for an entire generation of Americans. Set against the mythic backdrop of the American West (mythic in more ways than one: Rogers grew up in a Cincinnati tenement, though he had Choctaw blood in his veins), they embodied an ideal of gentle strength and homespun wisdom. ● "A little song, a little riding, a little shooting, and a girl to be saved from hazard" was Rogers' summary of the formula that made them both stars. Autry came first, rising to the top in radio, film, and records. (The gimmick of christening top records *gold* or *platinum* was invented to honor Autry's unprecedented sales, and his "Rudolph, the Red-Nosed Reindeer" remains the second-biggest single of all time.) When he got bogged down in contract disputes with Republic Pictures and then enlisted for WWII, Rogers, a bit player in Autry's films, rose to top billing. Eventually, Westerns fell out of favor, but both celluloid cowboys had long since moved on, eventually amassing huge personal fortunes through investments. ● Rogers went first, on July 6. The last words he uttered, overheard by a nurse, were reported to have been "Well, Lord, it's been a long, hard ride." ● As for Autry, the only entertainer with five stars on the Hollywood Walk of Fame, he had one last dream to fulfill: to see the team he bought in 1961, the California Angels, go to the World Series. It wasn't meant to be. After a long illness, and less than a week after the Angels lost their play-off bid, Autry died, on Oct. 2. To the end, friends said, he remained true to his personal code: "Never shoot first. Never go back on your word. Keep clean in thought, speech, action, and personal habits. Be gentle with children, the elderly, and animals." —M M F

"WHERE DO GENERALS KEEP their armies?" Shari Lewis once asked her most famous creation, Lamb Chop. And, as if it were the most obvious thing in the world, the puppet replied, "In their *sleevies!*" Such enchanting silliness was Lewis' stock-in-trade. "I have always believed in innocent excitement," she once said. "Magic, stunts, music, and riddles instead of explosions, crashes, and chases." • That philosophy—which Lewis displayed in skits on *Captain Kangaroo*, on her own popular Saturday-morning '60s kids' show, and in countless books and videos—would earn her a dozen Emmys, seven Parent's Choice Awards, and a Peabody. • When Lewis was diagnosed with uterine cancer last summer, she was taping a new PBS series, *The Charlie Horse Music Pizza*. "She found out on a Wednesday at 11 a.m.," said her daughter, Mallory Tarcher, "and was at rehearsal at 1 p.m." Within six weeks, she was gone. Until the end, Lewis never lost touch with her young fans. At a 1998 tribute dinner, a little girl silently walked up and hugged Lewis' knees under the table. Lewis explained her bond with kids this way: "I never play teacher. I never play parent. I play older playmate." —MMF

CARL WILSON | born 1946

ANY TRUE BEACH BOYS FAN knows that the flip side to the California-based group's sun-and-fun paeans lay in wistful tunes like "God Only Knows" and "Wouldn't It Be Nice," both sung by Carl Wilson. But if his voice was famed as the soul of Beach Boys music, it was less well known that Wilson's soothing persona was what united the group. "He never wanted credit for their success," recalled cousin Stan Love, "but he was the glue that held the band together." He was also a fighter: Diagnosed with lung cancer in March 1997, Wilson still joined the band for its 36th annual tour that summer. When he succumbed last Feb. 6 at age 51, he left Brian as the sole surviving sibling of the three brothers who had cofounded the band in 1961 (Dennis drowned in 1983). He also left a hole in the heart of anyone who'd ever marveled at his angelic voice. Either alone or raised in harmony, it was an instrument of sublime, heartrending purity. —TOM SINCLAIR

E.G. MARSHALL | born 1910

ULYSSES S. GRANT. Dwight D. Eisenhower. Harry S. Truman. Was there any other actor who could so convincingly play Commanders-in-Chief? Stern and impressive, E.G. Marshall spent his five-decade film and TV career portraying what he called "establishment daddies," but Marshall described himself as a "utility actor" who took easily to any role requiring an authoritative voice or somber visage. Ironically, Marshall's two Emmys came from his role as daringly antiestablishment attorney Lawrence Preston in CBS' dramatic 1960s courtroom series *The Defenders*, whose cases involved such then-taboo topics as abortion, euthanasia, and the blacklist. Marshall's willingness to tackle thorny issues, however, didn't shed any light on the mystery of what his initials stood for. At different times, he deciphered them as Everett G., Edda Gunnar, and (jokingly) Egregious Gregarious. Which was it? Said son-in-law David Saye: "It will go with him to his grave." —CWC

BETTY CARTER | born 1930

"AN AUDIENCE MAKES ME THINK, makes me reach for things I'd never try in the studio," Betty Carter once said of what drove her astounding stage performances. The self-proclaimed "Godmother of Jazz," who endured decades of obscurity rather than bend her art to popular taste, died of pancreatic cancer in Brooklyn on Sept. 26. • Carter's commercial apogee was probably her 1961 duet album with Ray Charles, which featured a hit version of "Baby, It's Cold Outside." But it was on stage, where she partnered with Charlie Parker, Dizzy Gillespie, and Miles Davis, that the songstress truly took flight. An improvisational scat genius who used her voice as an instrument, Carter became to jazz vocals what John Coltrane and Thelonious Monk were to instrumentation. She also made it her mission to incubate new jazz talent, first at the Brooklyn Academy of Music, then at Washington's Kennedy Center (Carter's work earned her a 1997 National Medal of Arts). She even featured many of her prodigies on the 1988 album *Look What I Got!*, which earned her a Grammy for Best Female Jazz Vocalist. It seems the Grammy voters had finally caught on to what jazz legend Carmen McRae always knew: "There's really only one jazz singer. Only one. Betty Carter." —M.M.F

JACK LORD | born 1920

ON SCREEN, dour Steve McGarrett ruled the *Hawaii Five-O* squad with an iron hand. Behind the cameras, Jack Lord was even more firmly in control. "He was a strict taskmaster, a perfectionist," recalled Kam Fong, who played Det. Chin Ho Kelly on the hit '70s TV series. Still, Fong added, "he was a softy, but he didn't want anybody to know it." He was also a man with a serious artistic side: Born John Joseph Patrick Ryan in 1920, Lord displayed such surprising talent as a painter that his canvases have been displayed in major museums and galleries. But a stint in the merchant marine led to roles in some training films, and Lord moved on to Broadway, bit parts in Hollywood, and, in 1968, Honolulu. (The series so boosted Hawaii's economy that Lord was considered the honorary mayor of Honolulu, where a day was named in his honor.) "This show will be it for me," proclaimed the man whose Cadillac had *Hawaii Five-O* license plates. "I'll never leave the islands. They'll have to carry me out." —CWC

LLOYD BRIDGES | born 1913

LLOYD BRIDGES GOT HIS FIRST TASTE of fame in 1913, when President Taft awarded him a trophy as America's fattest baby. He didn't rate much serious public notice again until 1952, when a series of tough-guy roles led him to play the weaselly deputy who skunks out on Gary Cooper's sheriff in *High Noon*. But it was later in that decade that the robust, craggy actor landed his most indelible early part, playing an underwater crime solver on TV's *Sea Hunt*. By the '80s and '90s, Bridges was turning that no-nonsense image on its head, letting out his inner goof in a succession of movies (*Airplane!*, *Hot Shots!*, *Mafia!*) and on TV's *Seinfeld*. He was also gaining fame for a far different role: beloved patriarch to a burgeoning acting family (including sons Jeff and Beau) that was, by Hollywood standards, rare in its closeness. "That's what was important to him," Beau said after his father's death. "That's what we remember about him." One of the many lessons Bridges imparted to his sons about acting (and life) was this simple truth: "If you're doing something you really love, you can do it forever." —JN

FLIP WILSON | born 1933

"I ACCOMPLISHED WHAT I set out to do" was how Flip Wilson, who died on Nov. 25, explained walking away from his TV show in 1975 while it was still in the top 10. Network TV's first black superstar (he won two Emmys and made TIME's cover in 1972) was leaving to spend more time with his children. Or, as he put it, to "make sure they don't go through what I did." Clerow Wilson had been born into grinding poverty (he once recalled that "my happiest memory of childhood was my first birthday in reform school") and quit school at age 16 to join the Air Force, where his quick wit earned him the nickname "Flip." Later, while working as a bellhop, he persuaded a San Francisco hotel manager to let him go on stage while the main act was on break; from then on, Wilson was a regular. After talk-show appearances earned him a steady following, Wilson got his own variety show in 1970. His parade of characters (including the sassy Geraldine, of whom Wilson once said, "She carried me longer than my mother did") and catchphrases ("Heah come de judge!" or "The devil made me do it!") caught on quickly with both white and black audiences, proving Wilson's dictum that "funny is not a color." Indeed, the secret of Wilson's appeal may have been (to borrow a phrase he made famous) that what we saw was what we got. —MMF

CARL PERKINS | born 1932

THIS SON OF A SHARECROPPER, who came to music at age 7 when his father made him a guitar out of a cigar box, a broomstick, and some baling wire, wrote his biggest hit, "Blue Suede Shoes," on the back of a potato sack in a Tennessee housing project. Of that song, he recalled, "God said, 'I've held it back, but this is it. Now you get down and get it.'" Perkins got it: The tune became part of the rock & roll canon, and the musical savant, who along with Elvis originated the pounding, rhythmic style of guitar that was to be the backbone of rock, was admired by legions of music giants, from the Beatles to Eric Clapton to Bob Dylan. Mega-fame eluded him, but Perkins (who died of a stroke on Jan. 19, at age 65) didn't mind: "People say, 'What happened to you, Carl? All of them went on to superstardom. Where'd you go?' I say, 'I went home.' And that's a good place to be." Inducted into the Rock and Roll Hall of Fame in 1987, Perkins leaves behind a legacy of great tunes, an indomitable spirit (he battled back from alcoholism in 1968), and a joyously swinging epitaph: "Go, Cat, Go!" —TS

RODDY MCDOWALL | born 1928

WITH HIS PRIMITIVE TURN in the classic *Planet of the Apes*, Roddy McDowall informed Cornelius, the simian sociologist, with the same earnest tenderness with which he lived. Born in London to a merchant seaman father and a stage mother, McDowall vaulted his way to fame at the age of 12 in such film classics as John Ford's *How Green Was My Valley* and *Lassie Come Home*. His arc might have been as brief as the typical child star's but for a dogged persistence that led to a second career as a character actor in more than 100 films and TV shows (he won a Tony for *The Fighting Cock* and an Emmy for NBC's *Not Without Honor*). McDowall survived as an actor, but he became legendary as a famous friend to many famous friends, from Elizabeth Taylor to Johnny Depp. "I've had a life crowded by incident and spotted with fascinating individuals," the studiously discreet actor once said. "I'll just keep the stories to myself." But if he was closemouthed about what he heard, McDowall generously shared what he saw: He became a respected portrait photographer, publishing four books of candid shots of his closest pals. Not long before succumbing to cancer on Oct. 3, at age 70, McDowall told one friend, Carol Burnett: "I have been battling something I cannot win, and I am withdrawing from the field with honor." —MARC BERNARDIN

TAMMY WYNETTE | born 1942

"I WRITE BETTER WHEN I'M DEPRESSED," Tammy Wynette once said. And life provided her an endless supply of material: four divorces, 30 operations, shock therapy, bankruptcy, drug addiction, a kidnapping, and a near shooting (by reportedly coked-up third husband George Jones, who chased her around their Florida mansion with a rifle). • She poured all of that misery into music, turning herself into a spokesperson for long-suffering women everywhere. "I can relate to any woman because I've worked in a shoe factory, been a barmaid, a waitress, and worked in a garment factory," said Wynette, who died on April 6. So closely did she identify with her audience that this ex-beautician even kept her license current until the end of her life. • Born to a rural Mississippi family so poor she is said to have made her clothing out of flour sacks, Wynette was, by age 17, already trapped in a bad marriage and caring for a child with spinal meningitis. She sought escape in her music, fantasizing about becoming a country singer. "Dream on, baby," Wynette's first husband answered, "dream on." • But her 1968 breakout hit, "Stand By Your Man," became the best-selling single ever recorded by a female country artist, and Wynette would go on to sell more than 30 million records, producing 21 No. 1 singles. • "I've had a wonderful life," Wynette looked back and said. "I've been blessed tremendously." She put it another way when her first husband approached her years after their divorce and asked her to autograph a photo. "Dream on, baby," she wrote. "Dream on."

ROBERT YOUNG | born 1907

HE IS REMEMBERED most for playing the ideal dad and the perfect doctor, both of whom really *did* seem to know best. As Jim Anderson on *Father Knows Best*, Young was the ultimate '50s suburban pop. He later said he was playing the father he had always wanted, rather than the cold, distant one he had grown up with, and the role earned him two Emmys. When Young returned to TV in 1969, he was determined to play Marcus Welby, M.D., as an equally reassuring character. The show brought Young a third Emmy—and gave ABC its first No. 1 hit. But the benign public image had a dark parallel: Beneath that avuncular demeanor was a man haunted by alcoholism and depression (he attempted suicide in 1991). Still, there was more truth in his roles than perhaps even Young (who died on July 21) understood. As Lauren Chapin, who played youngest daughter Kitten on *Father Knows Best*, recalled: "He took care of me.... He was the father I never had." A whole generation felt the same way. —J N

MAUREEN O'SULLIVAN | born 1911

SHE WAS BEST KNOWN FOR PLAYING the scantily clad Jane in *Tarzan* movies and for being Mia Farrow's mother. But Maureen O'Sullivan loathed her simian costar ("Cheetah, that bastard, bit me whenever he could") and considered herself too old to play Mia's mom in *Hannah and Her Sisters* ("But Mother," Farrow is said to have reminded her, "you *are* my mother"). Discovered by a Twentieth Century Fox director at a dance in Ireland, O'Sullivan, the daughter of a British army officer, was brought to America at age 20. Despite a burgeoning film career that included not only the *Tarzan* pictures but also classics like *Anna Karenina* and *Pride and Prejudice*, she had no pretensions about her acting. "They raved about my agonized look and the tears in my eyes," she said of a death scene in George Cukor's *David Copperfield*, "but it was all because George was twisting my feet off camera." She brought the same clear-eyed view to real life. When daughter Mia (one of seven kids O'Sullivan had with writer-director John Farrow) was contemplating marriage to Frank Sinatra in 1966, O'Sullivan quipped, "At his age, he should marry me!" But O'Sullivan, who died on June 22, wasn't always so sharp-tongued: "If you live generously without concentrating on yourself," she once said, "you'll become lovely through an inner beauty." —MMF

Esther Rolle

ESTHER ROLLE / born 1920 One of 18 siblings who grew up on a Southern farm, Rolle based her portrayal of Florida (the maid on *Maude* who was spun off to her own series, *Good Times*, in 1974) on one of her aunts. Ever principled, Rolle (who died Nov. 17 of diabetes) quit the show when she felt it was becoming demeaning to African Americans (though she later returned), and went on to win an Emmy in 1979 (for *Summer of My German Soldier*).

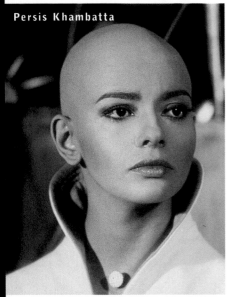

Persis Khambatta

PHILIP ABBOTT, 74, TV actor (*The FBI*); Feb. 23

BOB "TEX" ALLEN, 92, Western film star; Oct. 9

ERIC AMBLER, 89, Oscar-winning screenwriter, novelist; Oct. 22

CLEVELAND AMORY, 81, author and TV critic; Oct. 14

A. STERL ARTLEY, 91, author (*Dick and Jane* series); July 7

MARSHALL BARER, 75, lyricist (*Once Upon a Mattress*, *Mighty Mouse* theme); Aug. 25

EVA BARTOK, 72, actress (*The Crimson Pirate*); Aug. 1

LAURIE BEECHMAN, 43, actress (Grizabella in *Cats*); March 8

OWEN BRADLEY, 82, Nashville music producer; Jan. 7

BUDDY, 10, golden retriever in *Air Bud*; Feb. 11

LEO BUSCAGLIA, 74, self-help author known as Dr. Love; June 12

JERRY NEAL CAPEHEART, 69, songwriter ("Summertime Blues"); June 9

HARRY CARAY, 78, baseball sportscaster; Feb. 18

HELEN CARTER, 70, country-music legend; June 2

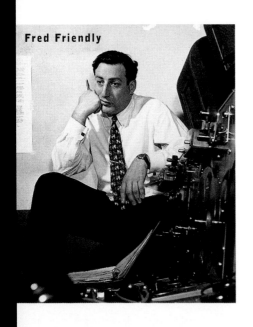

Fred Friendly

RICHARD CASSILLY, 70, tenor opera star; Jan. 30

CARLOS CASTANEDA, 72, best-selling anthropological author; April 27

JOSEPH CATES, 74, TV producer (*The $64,000 Question*); Oct. 10

KACEY CISYK, 44, commercial jingle singer; March 29

DANE CLARK, 85, actor, self-described Joe Average; Sept. 11

HENRY STEELE COMMAGER, 95, historian, author, teacher, antiwar activist; March 2

DONALD CONROY, 77, father of Pat and inspiration for *The Great Santini*; May 9

RICHARD DENNING, 84, actor (*An Affair to Remember*, *Some Like It Hot*, *Hawaii Five-O*); Oct. 11

JOHN DEREK, 71, actor-director, husband of Bo Derek, and ex of Linda Evans and Ursula Andress; May 22

WALTER DIEMER, 93, creator of bubble gum; Jan. 8

WADE DOMINGUEZ, 32, actor (*Dangerous Minds*); Aug. 26

DOROTHY DONEGAN, 76, jazz pianist; May 19

O'LANDA DRAPER, 34, Grammy-nominated gospel singer; July 21

JIMMY DRIFTWOOD, 91, Grammy-winning folk crooner; July 12

Alice Faye

Eddie Rabbitt

ALLEN DRURY, 80,
author (*Advise and Consent*);
Sept. 2

GENE EVANS, 75,
actor (*My Friend Flicka*);
April 1

FALCO, 40,
Austrian new-wave hitmaker;
Feb. 7

ALICE FAYE, 86,
box office star of the late '30s
and early '40s; May 9

GENE FOWLER, 80,
director (*I Was a Teen-age
Werewolf*); May 11

MARY FRANN, 55,
actress (Bob Newhart's wife on
Newhart); Sept. 23

FRED FRIENDLY, 82,
former president of CBS News;
March 3

MARTHA GELLHORN, 89,
war correspondent, novelist,
Hemingway's third wife;
Feb. 15

JAMES GOLDMAN, 71,
playwright, screenwriter (*The
Lion in Winter*); Oct. 28

HENRY HAMPTON, 58,
Emmy-winning documentary
filmmaker (*Eyes on the Prize*);
Nov. 22

RODNEY HARVEY, 30,
actor (*My Own Private Idaho*);
April 10

JOHN HAWKES, 72,
postmodern novelist; May 15

JOAN HICKSON, 92,
actress (lead in TV's *Miss
Marple*); Oct. 17

LILLIAN HOBAN, 73,
illustrator (the *Frances* children's books), author; July 17

JOHN HOLLIMAN, 49,
CNN correspondent; Sept. 12

TED HUGHES, 68,
British poet laureate, ex-hus-
band of Sylvia Plath; Oct. 28

MEGS JENKINS, 81,
British actress known for
"mom" roles; Oct. 5

BOB KANE, 83,
Batman creator; Nov. 3

TIMOTHY KELLY, 34,
guitarist for early-'90s metal
band Slaughter; Feb. 5

Mary Frann

NORMAN FELL / born 1925
Best known for playing the puri-
tanical-but-leering landlord on
TV's *Three's Company* (and on
his spin-off, *The Ropers*), Fell,
who died on Dec. 14, also had
an accomplished film career,
appearing in *The Graduate* (as
Dustin Hoffman's grumpy landlord), *Ocean's Eleven*, *Inherit
the Wind*, and, more recently,
For the Boys. But over the
years, when fans met him on the
street, "Mr. Roper" was inev-
itably the name they called out.

Norman
Fell

PERSIS KHAMBATTA, 49,
actress (*Star Trek: The Motion
Picture*); Aug. 18

**DAVID "JUNIOR"
KIMBROUGH**, 67,
influential blues musician;
Jan. 17

LEONID KINSKEY, 95,
actor (bartender in
Casablanca); Sept. 8

PHIL LEEDS, 82,
actor (judge on *Ally McBeal*);
Aug. 23

FREDERICK LENZ, 48,
New Age guru, author
(*Surfing the Himalayas*);
April 13

John
Derek

Junior Wells

Mae Questel

Dr. Benjamin Spock

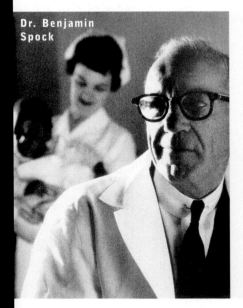

JOSEPH MAHER, 64,
stage, film, and TV actor;
July 17

JEAN MARAIS, 84,
French actor (Jean Cocteau's
Beauty and the Beast); Nov. 8

ROBERT MARASCO, 62,
playwright (*Child's Play*); Dec. 6

DANIEL MASSEY, 64,
actor, son of Raymond;
March 25

GEORGE MASTERS, 62,
makeup artist (for Marilyn
Monroe, and for Dustin
Hoffman in *Tootsie*); March 6

BOB MERRILL, 77,
songwriter (*Funny Girl*, "How
Much Is That Doggie in the
Window?"); Feb. 17

THERESA MERRITT, 75,
actress (*That's My Mama*);
June 12

JAY MONAHAN, 42,
NBC legal analyst, husband of
Katie Couric; Jan. 24

CORBETT MONICA, 68,
comedian, Rat Pack sidekick;
July 22

WRIGHT MORRIS, 88,
award-winning writer-
photographer; April 25

JEFFREY MOSS, 56,
cocreator of *Sesame Street*,
composer of "Rubber Duckie";
Sept. 24

JIM MURRAY, 78,
L.A. Times sportswriter;
Aug. 16

**DR. BENJAMIN SPOCK /
born 1903**   Only God sold
more books. America's parenting guru amassed some amazing
stats with his *Baby and Child
Care*: 50 million copies, 42 languages, 7 editions, and the No. 2
U.S. sales spot (after the Bible).
"What I tried to tell parents,"
he said, "is that it's okay to love
your child." But the "permis-
sive" rap was wide of the mark:
Spock (who died on March 15)
deemed videogames "a colossal
waste of time." —c w c

Buffalo Bob Smith

JEANETTE NOLAN, 86,
character actress (*The Horse
Whisperer*); June 5

DICK O'NEILL, 70,
actor (Cagney's dad on *Cagney
& Lacey*); Nov. 17

OCTAVIO PAZ, 84,
Nobel Prize-winning novelist;
April 19

STEPHEN PEARLMAN, 63,
actor (*Law & Order*); Sept. 30

LEO PENN, 77,
blacklist survivor, TV director,
father of Sean and Chris;
Sept. 5

ROB PILATUS, 32,
half of pop hoaxters Milli
Vanilli; April 3

SHIRLEY POVICH, 92,
legendary *Washington Post*
sports columnist, father of
Maury; June 4

COZY POWELL, 50,
drummer (Black Sabbath,
Whitesnake, Rainbow); April 5

ANTONIO PROHIAS, 77,
cartoonist (*Mad* magazine's
"Spy vs. Spy" series); Feb. 24

MAE QUESTEL, 89,
voice of Betty Boop and Olive
Oyl; Jan. 4

EDDIE RABBITT, 56,
country singer ("I Love a Rainy
Night," "Drivin' My Life
Away"); May 7

GENE RAYMOND, 89,
'30s and '40s movie star;
May 3

HUGH REILLY, 82,
actor (dad on TV's *Lassie*);
July 17

BOB RUSSELL, 90,
cocreator of *Name That Tune*,
ex–Miss America host; Jan. 24

DAVE "CHICO" RYAN, 50,
member of Sha Na Na; July 29

LEONIE RYSANEK, 71,
soprano opera star; March 7

STEVE SANDERS, 45,
former guitarist of the Oak
Ridge Boys; June 10

TAZIO SECCHIAROLI, 73,
inspiration for the *La Dolce Vita*
character Paparazzo; July 24

ATISON KEN SEIULI, 21,
transsexual prostitute spotted
with Eddie Murphy; April 22

SIDNEY SIMIEN, 59,
zydeco musician; Feb. 25

EMIL SITKA, 83,
character actor (*The Three
Stooges* movies); Jan. 19

BUFFALO BOB SMITH, 80,
Howdy Doody host; July 30

ROGER L. STEVENS, 87,
Broadway producer (*West Side
Story, A Man for All Seasons,
Deathtrap*); Feb. 2

DOROTHY STICKNEY, 101,
stage legend; June 2

KAY THOMPSON, 95,
creator of *Eloise*; July 2

SIR MICHAEL TIPPETT, 93,
British composer; Jan. 8

BOB TROW, 72,
actor (Bob Dog from *Mister
Rogers' Neighborhood*); Nov. 2

Rob
Pilatus

J.T. WALSH / born 1944
Though he didn't start performing until age 30, Walsh became one of the best character actors of his generation. A journeyman who specialized in banal bad guys, Walsh (who died on Feb. 27) strove to convey "just how ordinary and everyday real evil is" in films like *Breakdown* and *A Few Good Men*. This master of understated menace had a term for creepy characters like the pervert he played in *Sling Blade*: "ethically challenged."

J.T. Walsh

SYLVIA FIELD TRUEX, 97,
actress (Mrs. Wilson on TV's
Dennis the Menace);
July 31

HELEN WARD, 82,
Big Band singer; April 21

STEVE WASSERMAN, 45,
TV producer (*Beverly Hills
90210*); July 3

BENNY WATERS, 96,
hepcat nonpareil; Aug. 11

JUNIOR WELLS, 63,
blues master; Jan. 15

DOROTHY WEST, 91,
Harlem Renaissance writer;
Aug. 16

ROZZ WILLIAMS, 34,
Goth singer with band Christian
Death; April 1

WENDY O. WILLIAMS, 48,
former lead singer of punk band
Plasmatics; April 6

BEATRICE WOOD, 105,
artist who inspired *Titanic*'s
Rose; March 12

MARVIN WORTH, 72,
producer (*Lenny, The Rose,
Malcolm X*); April 22

FREDDIE YOUNG, 96,
Oscar-winning cinematographer
(*Lawrence of Arabia*);
Dec. 1

HENNY YOUNGMAN, 91,
snappy comic; Feb. 24

MICHAEL ZASLOW, 54,
Emmy award-winning soap
actor; Dec. 6

Wendy O.
Williams

Henny
Youngman

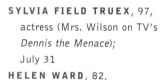

photocredits

> **COVERS/FRONT OF BOOK** Hanks: Nigel Parry/CPI; Diaz: photograph by Andrew Southam; Backstreet Boys: George Holz/Outline; DiCaprio: Greg Gorman/Outline; Flockhart: photograph by Robert Erdmann; Seinfeld: Stephen Danelian/Outline; Roberts: Albert Sanchez/Outline; Damon: photograph by Mark Hanauer; agency: Beauty & Photo; Ryan: Outline; Spade: photograph by Sam Jones; Hill: Amanda Searle; Sinatra: (hardcover) Phil Stern/CPI; Sinatra: (softcover) Ted Allan/MPTV; page opposite masthead, Imbruglia: Martyn Thompson/ESP; Busta Rhymes: Timothy White/Outline; Sandler: Joshua Jordan

> **THE ENTERTAINERS** THE TOP 12, page 8: Cliff Watts/Icon International; 15: Joshua Jordan; 16: Davis Factor/Outline; 22: Warren du Preez/British *GQ*/Condé Nast; BREAKOUT STARS, page 29: Tim Brett Day/Celebrity Pictures UK; 32: Caroline Greyshock; BEST OF REST, page 36: Visages; 39: Michael Lavine (3); 43: Outline

> **THE YEAR IN REVIEW** MOMENTS, page 54: Mary Ellen Matthews; 55: (top) L.M. Otero/AP/Wide World; Gamma Liaison; 56: (top) photograph by Henny Garfunkel; Margaret Norton; 57: (right) Mark Lennihan/AP/Wide World (3); 59: (top) News International; Marc Bryan Brown; 60: Nina Prommer/Globe Photos; 61: (clockwise from top left) Susan Sterner/AP/Wide World; Rene Marcura/AP/Wide World; Susan Sterner/AP/Wide World (2); Mark J. Terrill/AP/Wide World; 63: (top) Joey Del Valle; Stephane Cardinale/Sygma; 64: (top) AP/Wide World; Greg Gibson/AP/Wide World; 65: Bruce McBroom; 67: (top) Jeff Geissler/AP/Wide World; Bill Davila/Retna, Ltd.; 68: (top) Craig Blankenhorn; MSI/Sygma; 69: *National Enquirer*; 70: Mario Magnani/Gamma Liaison; 71: Don Ryan/AP/Wide World; 72: (bottom, clockwise from top left) Kevork Djansezian/AP/Wide World; Reed Saxon/AP/Wide World; Kevork Djansezian/AP/Wide World (3); 73: (top) photograph by Anthony Verde; (inset) Frank Trapper/Sygma; Terry Williams/London Features; 74: Brendan Beirne/Rex USA; 75: (top) Andy King/Sygma; 76: (top) DS/London Features; Arnaldo Magnani/Gamma Liaison; 77: (left) Susan Ragan/AP/Wide World; CBS News/AP/Wide World; BEHIND THE SCENES, page 78: David Hume Kennerly from *Sein Off*/HarperCollins; 81: Francois Duhamel; 83: Ken Regan/Camera 5; 84: John Seakwood; 85: Sam Erickson; 86: (top) Ken Regan/Camera 5; Stephen Vaughan; 87: Mary Ellen Mark; 88: Larry Fink; STYLE 1998, page 92: Los Angeles *Daily News*/Sygma; 93: (left) Stephane Cardinale/Sygma; Fitzroy Barrett/Globe Photos; 94: (clockwise from top left) Laszlo/Comedia (2); Kevin Mazur (3); 95: (from left) Janet Gough/Celebrity Photo; Jim Smeal/Galella, Ltd.; Barry King/Magnolia Press; Peter Kramer/Galella, Ltd.; 96: (clockwise from top left) Jim Spellman/IPOL; Steve Azzara/Sygma; Jim Smeal/Galella, Ltd.; Steve Azzara/Sygma; Janet Gough/Celebrity Photo; 97: (clockwise from top left) Gregory Pace/Sygma (3); Allan Tannenbaum/Sygma; 98: (clockwise from top left) Gilbert Flores/Celebrity Photo; Steve Azzara/Sygma; Frank Trapper/Sygma; 99: (clockwise from top left) Gilbert Flores/Celebrity Photo; Gregory Pace/Sygma; Celebrity Photo; Kathy Hutchins/Hutchins Photo (3); Kevin Mazur; Steve Finn/Globe Photos; Frank Trapper/Sygma; 100: (clockwise from top left) London Features; Laszlo/Comedia; Kevin Mazur; Roger Karnbad/Celebrity Photo; 101: Paul Smith/Retna, Ltd.; John Spellman/Retna, Ltd.; Big Pictures; Kevin Mazur; Barry Talesnick/Retna, Ltd.; P.A.G./Stills/Retna, Ltd.; 102: (clockwise from top left) Rose Hartman/Globe Photos; Paul Smith/Retna, Ltd. (2); Remy K/Hutchins Photo; Jim Smeal/Galella, Ltd.; Gilbert Flores/Celebrity Photo; Jim Smeal/Galella, Ltd.; Steve Granitz/Retna, Ltd.; 103: (clockwise from top left) Bill Davila/Retna, Ltd.; Paul Smith/Retna, Ltd.; Kevin Mazur; Steve Finn/Alpha/Globe Photos; Evan Agostini/Gamma Liaison; Jan Leonardo/Mazur (2); Lisa Rose/Globe Photos

> **BOWING OUT** page 125: © Herman Leonard; 126: Michael Ochs Archive; 127: Stephen Harvey/Outline; 128: Roger Ressmeyer/Corbis; 129: Everett Collection; 130: (from top) Globe Photos; Louis Goldman; 131: (from left) Richard Miller/MPTV; The Kobal Collection; 132: (from top) Photofest; Julian Wasser/LIFE; 133: Stu Smith/Globe Photos; 134: Tom Copi/Michael Ochs Archive; 135: (from top) Everett Collection; Photofest; 136: (from top) NBC/Globe Photos; Chuck Krall/Michael Ochs Archive; 137: Photofest; 138: (from top) Epic Records/Neal Peters Collection; Photofest; 139: Lester Glassner/Neal Peters Collection; 140: (from top) Gabi Rona/MPTV; Everett Collection; NBC; Ted Allan/MPTV; 141: (from top) Andy Freeberg/Retna, Ltd.; Photofest; Everett Collection; Tony Costa/Outline; 142: (from top) Everett Collection; Danny Clinch; Photofest; John Rees/Black Star; 143: (from top) Len Irish/Outline; Photofest; Marvin Newman; Michael Putland/Retna, Ltd.; this page: Lawrence Schwartzwald/Sygma